ORANGE THROWER

KIRSTY MARILLIER

CURRENCY PRESS
The performing arts publisher

**GRIFFIN
THEATRE
COMPANY**

CURRENT THEATRE SERIES

First published in 2022
by Currency Press Pty Ltd,
PO Box 2287, Strawberry Hills, NSW, 2012, Australia
enquiries@currency.com.au
www.currency.com.au

in association with Griffin Theatre Company.

Typeset by Brighton Gray for Currency Press.
Cover shows Kirsty Marillier.
Cover image by Brett Boardman, cover design by Alphabet.

Currency Press acknowledges the Traditional Owners of the Country on which
we live and work. We pay our respects to all Aboriginal and Torres Strait
Islander Elders, past and present.

A catalogue record for this
book is available from the
National Library of Australia

NATIONAL
LIBRARY
OF AUSTRALIA

Contents

ORANGE THROWER   1

Glossary   57

Theatre Program at the end of the playtext

For my Coloured fam.

Orange Thrower was first produced by Griffin Theatre Company at the SBW Stables, Darlinghurst, on 18 February, 2022, with the following cast:

ZADIE	Gabriela Van Wyk
VIMSY	Mariama Whitton
LEROY / SHARRON	Callan Colley
STEKKIE / PAUL	Angela Nica Sullen

Director, Zindzi Okenyo
Designer, Jeremy Allen
Lighting Designer, Verity Hampson
Associate Lighting Designer, Veronique Benett
Composer and Sound Designer, Benjamin Pierpoint
Dramaturg, Declan Greene
Directing Secondment, Chemon Theys
Stage Manager, Hannah Crane

The playwright would like to acknowledge and pay my respect to the traditional owners of Country on which this play was written. Elders past, present and emerging, the Wurundjeri people of the Kulin nation and the Gadigal people of the Eora nation. ALWAYS WAS, ALWAYS WILL BE ABORIGINAL LAND.

STUKKIE
1. A slang South African term referring to a girl or someone's girlfriend. Derived from the Afrikaans term 'Stukkie' meaning 'little piece'.
'Stuk': Piece, part.
2. A hot chick who could be curvalicious/thick in a sexy way.

CHARACTERS

ZADIE PETERSON, 22 years old. She/her. Mixed race/coloured South African immigrant. Australian dialect.

VIMSY PETERSON, 17 years old. She/her. Mixed race/coloured South African immigrant, Zadie's sibling, works at Chook Treat. Australian dialect.

LEROY, 22 years old. He/him. African descent. Swimmer. Boy-next-door vibes. Australian dialect.

STEKKIE, 35 years old. She/her. Mixed race/coloured South African womxn. Otherworldly. Thick South African accent.

SHARRON, boomer. She/her. Caucasian. Neighbour on Paradise Street. Australian dialect.

PAUL, boomer. He/him. Caucasian. Neighbour on Paradise Street. Australian dialect.

PLACE

The aspirational home estate of Paradise.

The Peterson household—Zadie and Vimsy's home.

The Rec.

TIME

Summer holidays.

NOTES

SHARRON to be played by the same actor playing LEROY.

PAUL to be played by the same actor playing STEKKIE.

SCENE ONE

Sunday. Dead of night.

A house in the aspirational suburb of Paradise.

The windows are shut.

A cordless home phone rings. It rings and rings.

Finally, an answering machine.

YOLANDI: [*voiceover, from machine*] Hi there, you've reached the Peterson household of Yolandi,

ARNIE: [*voiceover, from machine*] Arnie,

VIMSY: [*voiceover, from machine*] Vimsy!

ZADIE: [*voiceover, from machine*] and Zadie.

YOLANDI: [*voiceover, from machine*] We're not at home right now but leave us a message and we'll call you back as quick as we can!

> *The voice of* YOLANDI—*Zadie and Vimsy's mother—echoes from the machine.*

Mmmmmmmmm no answer? Why so quiet? Assuming it's late and you're both in bed but I thought I'd try. How are things over there? We off to Durban tomorrow. The weather is … sublime. It's sublime here. Speaking of, I saw on the Googles it's quite hot there, ey? Zadie listen, I need you to promise me everything's in order. No riff raff. I've added you to the Paradise WhatsApp group so if anything, … listen, I'm getting hives thinking the kitchen is on fire, or the lawn is on fire, or worse, your sister is on fire!

If Vimsy tries to give you cheek just remember *you* are in charge this summer. [*Beat*] Anyways. There are sausages in the freezer, emergency numbers on the fridge, Sharron across the road knows you're alone. Okay, call your mama back, okay.

> *Suddenly something hits the house. It's loud.*
>
> *And again and again and again.*
>
> *Blackout.*

SCENE TWO

House. The next morning.

LEROY *is standing opposite* ZADIE, *who's wearing her summer PJs.*

LEROY *is wearing bright boardshorts, a backpack and a gold crucifix strung around his neck. He's holding three mangled oranges.*

ZADIE: Wait where?

LEROY: Out the front.

ZADIE: Out the front, where?

LEROY: Your porch. Near the—not *on* the welcome mat but near it, near the door.

ZADIE: Just sitting there?

LEROY: Three of them sitting splattered, yeah.

ZADIE: Weird …

>LEROY *looks down at the oranges.*

LEROY: [*handing them over to* ZADIE] Hey can you—?

ZADIE: Don'ttt give them to me—

LEROY: Well, I don't wanna—

ZADIE: *You* brought them in here!

LEROY: Is there like a bin? Can I throw them in your bin, please?

>ZADIE *grabs a bin.* LEROY *drops the oranges in.*

[*Shrieking*] Bleurgh! Manky.

>LEROY *wipes his hands on his shorts.* ZADIE *puts the bin away.*

Maybe some weirdo's tryna get your attention.

ZADIE: What?

LEROY: A guy.

ZADIE: Tryna to get my attention?

LEROY: Chyeah!

ZADIE: [*scoffing*] Ain't no *guy* in Paradise trying to get my attention, Leroy.

LEROY: You don't know that! I mean you don't know that for sure. And you never know Zadie, I've done some pretty crazy shiiit to get a chick to notice me and—

LEROY *catches* ZADIE*'s eye.*

So, what are you up to today?

ZADIE: What are *you* up to today?

LEROY: I have swimming in an / hour.

ZADIE: / Oh! At The Rec?

LEROY: Yeah! Actually reckon I could get changed here?

ZADIE: Changed?

LEROY: Some old guy got staph last week so the men's changerooms have been wigging me out.

ZADIE: Don't you have your flip-flops?

ZADIE *snorts.*

LEROY: Flip-flops?

ZADIE: Yeah! Remember when we were sixteen and you always used to wear those gross lime green flip-flops.

LEROY: [*mortified*] Oh …

ZADIE: And your toes! Remember how your toes couldn't sit flat? You had those … weird little speed bump toes—are they still like that!?

ZADIE *tries to check out his toes.* LEROY *ducks.*

LEROY: No, they're not!! Also, I don't wear those anymore! The green—

ZADIE: Oh.

LEROY: And I got orthotics for my hammertoes. In year twelve. Remember?

ZADIE: [*stifling a laugh*] Oh, yep, yep! I remember.

Sorry.

LEROY *loiters a moment.*

The spare room's free … if you wanna get changed.

LEROY *goes to get changed.*

ZADIE *walks over to the oranges.*

LEROY: [*from the other room*] So … am I gonna see you tonight?

ZADIE: [*to the other room*] Tonight?

LEROY: Martin's doof! Starts at four.

ZADIE: Oh I wasn't invite—yeah I have work.

LEROY: Damn. Assuming your sister will be there?

ZADIE: Vims? Ahh nah, it's not really her vibe.

LEROY: She was at the last one.

>ZADIE's *eyes widen.*

ZADIE: Was she …?

LEROY: That's why I came over actually, I saw her on the d-floor and ah … Ithoughtaboutya!

ZADIE: Right …

LEROY: It's been ages.

ZADIE: Since church Days.

LEROY: Ha! 'Church DayZz'.

ZADIE: Remember Father Tim's lisp? 'Peath be with you'.

LEROY: I still go.

ZADIE: Do you?

>LEROY *enters wearing fluoro orange speedos. His bod is toned and swimmer-like.*

LEROY: Courth I do.

>*A hot moment.*

ZADIE: [*recoiling*] So you train every day, right? Mum, she mentioned it.

LEROY: Pretty much. Most mornings.

ZADIE: Wow!

LEROY: I've got a comp next week.

ZADIE: Cool! Comps and stuff?

LEROY: It's small time but Olympic type goalz, girl!

ZADIE: Explains the speedos.

LEROY: Splains the speedos.

ZADIE: Bit of a garish colour, aren't they?

LEROY: They suit the infrastructure.

ZADIE: THHHHORPEEEEDOOO—Are you hungry? Or like thirsty? Do you want anything to drink?

LEROY: Youshouldcomeifyouwant.

>*Beat.*

ZADIE: Come if I want where?

LEROY: You should come.

ZADIE: When?

LEROY: Now. To The Rec. You should come with me now to *The Rec.*

ZADIE: OHHHHHHHH—

LEROY: Or you could meet me after? *After* training if you want? It's gonna be really hot today.

ZADIE: Yeah, your forehead is drenched.

LEROY: Is it?

LEROY *wipes his forehead.*

ZADIE: It's fine youlookhot—It is hot!—It's forty-fucking-degreesofcourseyou'rehot um yeah, I've actually got a bit of cleaning I've gotta do.

LEROY: Cleaning?

ZADIE: Yep! And I have a shift!

LEROY: What time's your shift?

ZADIE: In six hours.

They lock eyes.

LEROY: Fair enough.

LEROY *tries another angle.*

So, what do you reckon you're gonna do? You gonna tell the cops?

ZADIE: The cops???

LEROY: Yeah. About the / oranges.

ZADIE: / Oh! I didn't think it was—

LEROY: It's vandalism, Zadie.

Beat.

ZADIE: Vandalism?

LEROY: Yeah! I mean, just because it's fruit doesn't mean it's not—

ZADIE: Wait, you think someone threw / them?

LEROY: / It's kinda like some fuckin … *fruit* vandalism!

ZADIE: Fruit vandalism.

LEROY: Some vandal. In Paradise. Throwing shit fruit at your house!

ZADIE: Woah …

LEROY: While you're asleep!

ZADIE *stares into the bin.*

LEROY *walks closer to her.*

Yo … if it is … I could help you figure it out.

LEROY *gives a dreamy smile.*

ZADIE: And … how would you help me?

> LEROY *musters some courage.*

LEROY: Zadie … I'd love it if some time we could—

> *The phone rings. But these two seem kinda stuck.*

ZADIE: I should probably get / that.
LEROY: / You should probably get / that.
ZADIE: / It'll probably be Mum.
LEROY: Mum?
ZADIE: Yeah, Mum's been leaving these hectic anal voicemails since they—
LEROY: Where are they exactly?

> *The Petersons' answering machine.*

> *Then* SHARRON*'s voice is heard from the machine.*

SHARRON: [*voiceover, from machine*] Um yeah hi number 66. This is Sharron here from 65.

> ZADIE *breaks away from* LEROY *and races to the phone.*

We've actually noticed your …. bins weren't taken in this morning. Specifically, your yellow. If you could please—

> ZADIE *answers it.*

> *A sulky* LEROY *stomps over to his backpack, grabs his phone and scrolls.*

ZADIE: [*on the phone*] Sharron! Hi! Helloo. [*Beat*]
    Yes. The bins. Sorry, my sister, she's on bin duty but she must've— [*Beat*]
    Of course! I'll make sure she brings them in. Right now.

> ZADIE *puts her hand over the phone.*

[*Calling*] VIIIIMMMMMMMMMSSSS!
LEROY: Wait, is she seriously arking up about the—?
VIMSY: [*offstage*] WHATT??!
ZADIE: [*calling*] I literally told you to—
VIMSY: [*offstage*] Why are you yelling?
ZADIE: [*calling*] You didn't bring the bin in!
LEROY: [*to himself*] Gnarly …

VIMSY: [*offstage*] Which bin?

ZADIE: The *recycling*! Sharron across the road's on the phone.

> VIMSY *races in wearing her Chook Treat uniform and a gaming headset.*

VIMSY: Didn't your roster say Tuesday?

ZADIE: [*whispering*] It said Sunday!

VIMSY: Shit. Sorry.

LEROY: Heyy Vizz Fizz.

ZADIE: [*on the phone*] Sharron? Hi. So, Vimsy's gonna bring the bin / in.

VIMSY: / Zadie, I have work???

ZADIE: [*on the phone*] A-S-A-P! Absolutely!

LEROY: [*to* VIMSY] When's work?

VIMSY: [*to* LEROY] In ten minutes.

> VIMSY *spots the bus through the window.*

Shit! The bus!

LEROY: Oh yo, is it here!?

> VIMSY *frantically runs to her room.*

> LEROY *takes* ZADIE *in.*

ZADIE: [*on the phone*] Yep! Uhuh.

> *He makes the decision to put his backpack on.*

> VIMSY *beelines back in wearing her work cap. She guns for the door.*

VIMSY: [*sprinting*] Gottagogottagogottago!

LEROY: [*to* VIMSY] Oi Vims, you coming to Martin's doof?

> VIMSY *stops. Turns.*

VIMSY: Martin's. Nah. I have work. And an interviewww tomorrow.

LEROY: Bummer.

VIMSY: No doof. PS. You look good bro!

LEROY: [*bashful*] Thanks.

> ZADIE *puts her hand over the phone.*

ZADIE: Are you two going?

VIMSY: I've got work!

LEROY: Trainingg.

ZADIE: [*to* VIMSY] Hey your interview, tomorrow, it's at twelve.
VIMSY: [*leaving*] Yep, thankssss.
ZADIE: I printed off a map of the campus and—
VIMSY: Got ittt!

> VIMSY *leaves.*

> LEROY *goes to exit. Then stops. One last go.*

LEROY: [*to* ZADIE] Hey yo, Z!
ZADIE: [*on the phone*] One second, Sharron.
LEROY: Bin bidness aside. Vandalism aside. I got chu, yeah?
ZADIE: Ah …
LEROY: I'm one call away, bae!

> *The bus toots.*

VIMSY: [*from outside*] LEROY!
LEROY: Shit. [*To* ZADIE] Adios!

> LEROY *runs for the bus.*

ZADIE: Adios …

> ZADIE *watches* LEROY *go.*

> *Beat.*

[*On the phone*] Sharron! Sorry … about all that aha. [*Beat*]
No! The bins are all under control.
And there'll be no more surprises.
Promise.

> *As we transition:* ZADIE *grabs the bin with the oranges. She grimaces and exits outside.*

SCENE THREE

House. That night.

The windows are shut.

Outside, a white censor light turns on. A figure appears in the window. Large afro framed in synthetic light.

The figure slides open the window. It's STEKKIE.

Hair. Jeans. She's fucking fabulous.

STEKKIE *climbs into the house. She fumbles, falls.*
She straightens herself up. Fixes her fro. Still fabulous.
STEKKIE *gains her bearings. Takes in the house.*

STEKKIE: [*to herself*] Okay. Okay okay okay …

    STEKKIE *marvels at a shiny surface.*

Wow.

    The house alarm goes off.

    STEKKIE *freaks. Doesn't know what to do. She hides.*

    ZADIE *races in wearing her PJs. She runs over to a home control*
    security panel, types in a pin. It doesn't work.

ZADIE: Stupid!

    ZADIE *pins again.*

Flipping!

    And again.

Uggghh!!

    The alarm stops.

    ZADIE *clocks the window. It's open.*

    Then the home phone rings. ZADIE *quickly answers it.*

[*On the phone*] Hello? Oh. Hi Ma. [*Beat*] Yeah, no sorry the alarm
was—how did you kno—? [*Beat*] The WhatsApp group? Already?
Who messaged you? [*Beat*] Right …
What did she say? [*Beat*] … Right.

    STEKKIE *pokes her head out. She observes* ZADIE.

No, it was just the alarm. I think it's broken. Yes.

    STEKKIE *has a realisation.*

Sorry, I should've picked up before, I was in bed—sorry.

    ZADIE *notes the open window again.*

Hey Ma, can I call you back? Tomorrow? I just need to …
gotothebathroom. And it's late! Everything's okay now. The alarm's
off now. Stress less. Love you, Ma. Bye Ma.

ZADIE *hangs up.*

Walks over to the window. Looks out at the stillness of suburbia. Nothing.

ZADIE *shuts the window.*

STEKKIE *stealthily creeps up behind her. A wry smile on her face. She tickles* ZADIE.

STEKKIE: TICKLE TICKLE ZADIE DID A / TRICKLE!!!
ZADIE: / AAAHHH OHMYGODOHMYGOD!

STEKKIE *cracks up.*

OHMYGODOHMY/GOD!
STEKKIE: / Eish! Remember that / child?!
ZADIE: / OH MY GOD!
STEKKIE: 'Tickle tickle Zadie did a trickle!'
ZADIE: WHO ARE YOU—
STEKKIE: Every time you'd pee yourself!
ZADIE: WHY ARE YOU—
STEKKIE: 'Tickle trickle!' Eish SHIT MAN! I wasa FUCKIN BEAST with my comedy man can't believe I came up wit THAT CRAP—
ZADIE: Why are you in my house???
STEKKIE: Should've gotten into stand-up.
ZADIE: What do you want?!
STEKKIE: SHOHHHHHHH.

STEKKIE *puts her finger up to* ZADIE. *Commanding her.*

Stop your fretting, child. Why are you fretting for, huh? You going to give yourself lines, Zadie.

Beat.

ZADIE: How do you know my name?
STEKKIE: —
ZADIE: How'd you get in here?
STEKKIE: —
ZADIE: Mum and Dad. They aren't here. If you're here to see them.
STEKKIE: I'm … not here to see them.

Beat.

Where are they? Yolandi and Arnie.

ZADIE: In S.A. For the summer. You look familiar.

ZADIE's eyes adjust.

Ohhhhhhhhhh.

STEKKIE: [*smiling*] Yes 'oh'

ZADIE: *Ohhhhhhhhhhhhhhh—*

STEKKIE: Oh! Oh! Oh!

ZADIE: Stekkie?!

STEKKIE: Yah.

ZADIE: Stekkie. Wow. Wowwowwow hi. Hi you.

STEKKIE: Hi you.

ZADIE stands stunned.

You gonna keep standing there like a scared ass or you gonna come give me a kiss hello?

ZADIE walks up to STEKKIE. Hugs her. Breathes her in.

ZADIE: [*hugging her*] What are you doing here?

STEKKIE: [*hugging her*] You happy to see me?

ZADIE: Mmhm.

STEKKIE: Good. 'Cause I was thinking I could crash here.

ZADIE: Here?

STEKKIE: I looked on the Air Bnbs but there's nothing going so if I could perch here for a bit that would be nice.

ZADIE: Oh. Of course! You can perch as long you—how long do you think you'd need?

STEKKIE: As long as I need, don't worry I'll keep myself busy keep myself out of your hair—now tell me, what time's Vimsy be home?

ZADIE: Uh, Vims is out. At work.

STEKKIE: Ah. And where'z your dad keep his Jameson?

ZADIE: Uh, in the cupboard, above the splashback. But we're not allowed—

STEKKIE leaves the room in search of the cupboard above the splashback.

ZADIE has a moment. Scrunches her face. She surveys the room.

[*To* STEKKIE] Hey, where are your bags?

STEKKIE: [*from other room*] My word, nice pozzy y'all got.

ZADIE: [*to other room*] Pozzy?

> *Cupboards banging. Bottles clanging.*

STEKKIE: [*from other room*] 'Home', Zadie.

> ZADIE *checks out the window to see if anyone's outside.*

ZADIE: Oh. Yeah. Nice-ish

STEKKIE: Compared to back home very nice. Ver-y shiny.

> STEKKIE *re-enters. She has a bottle of whiskey and shot glass in hand.*

> ZADIE *turns. Smiles.*

ZADIE: IIII'm gonna pop you in the spare room. On the right at the end of the passage, Mum's got the good cotton in there—is that okay?

STEKKIE: Spare room's perfect, baba.

> STEKKIE *does a shot of whiskey.*

[*Under her breath*] Ah. Lekker.

> STEKKIE *leans back. Wipes sweat from her neck and breasts. An unsaid air of discomfort lingers.*

To be honest … I'll probably find a chap in this suburb, some eligible bachelor to knock boots with for a bit.

ZADIE: [*snorting*] I don't think there's anyone to 'knock boots' with in Paradise.

STEKKIE: Uh uh that's not true, I saw a young honey walking on the street, peeping round *this* house—who was that, huh?

ZADIE: Young honey?

STEKKIE: Teenie, tiny short shorts … ass cheeks like a god!

ZADIE: [*blushing*] Ahhh—

STEKKIE: He was cute, Zadie. Is he making you come, baby doll?

ZADIE: He's a friend!

STEKKIE: You been grabbing his long john?

ZADIE: Just a family frien—

STEKKIE: You been BUMPING AND GRINDING, huh?

> ZADIE *quickly shuts the window.*

Ohhhhhhh okay I'll be quiet. Be a quiet little mouse.

> STEKKIE *giggles.*

I'm sorry about the bed wetting comment before but it was funny, no?

ZADIE *gives* STEKKIE *a once over.*

ZADIE: It's late. I'm gonna head to bed but you're gonna be in the spare—

STEKKIE: Shoo! You got that commanding tone like your mother, huh?

ZADIE: [*spitting*] Does my *ma* know you're here?

STEKKIE*'s eyes go black.*

STEKKIE: Yolandi? No … Yolandi doesn't know I'm here but that's … ultra-fine.

ZADIE *tucks any frizz resembling* STEKKIE*'s behind her ear.* STEKKIE *notices.*

No need to be a sour lemon Zadie—

ZADIE: I'm not being a sour—

STEKKIE: I won't disrupt anything. Won't be a so called 'wayward'.

A heavy, loaded silence hangs between the two.

Suddenly something hits the house. It's loud.

ZADIE *and* STEKKIE *turn.*

ZADIE *walks towards the window. Opens it. Stillness of suburbia.*

What was that? Zadie?

ZADIE: I don't know …

STEKKIE: Is there anyone?

ZADIE: Hold on.

ZADIE *grabs a torch.*

STEKKIE: I'll come with you—

ZADIE: You stay.

She clicks on the torch.

I'll check it out.

ZADIE *exits. Leaves* STEKKIE *alone.*

STEKKIE: [*to herself*] Okay okay okay …

From her jeans pocket, STEKKIE *pulls out an old Motorola flip phone. She turns it on. Searches for range. The phone manically goes off.* STEKKIE *quickly turns it off.*

ZADIE re-enters. STEKKIE *hides her phone.*

ZADIE: Hey …
STEKKIE: Zadie what was it? Outside. What was that bang just now?
ZADIE: Um …
STEKKIE: You okay?
ZADIE: It was orange.

> *Neon light saturates the space.*
>
> *A thumping afro track plays.*
>
> *A little later,* VIMSY *creeps into the room.*
>
> *She's decked out in a teeny rave outfit with platform boots and winged eyeliner.*
>
> *A stark contrast to her fast-food reds.*
>
> VIMSY *pulls out a vape from her bra.*
>
> *She takes a puff,*
>
> *tiptoes across the house,*
>
> *and sneaks out.*

SCENE FOUR

House. The next morning.

VIMSY *beelines through wearing her Chook Treat uniform, platform rave boots and glitter.*

Next, STEKKIE *saunters through wearing a silk gown. They jussst miss each other.*

VIMSY *races back in wearing a nice, corporate outfit.*

She stops, caught ahead of STEKKIE.

STEKKIE: Where you off to, panda eyes?
VIMSY: … Hi … [*Beat*] Stekkie, right?
STEKKIE: I'll be honest it looks like you need some luving in the wardrobe department what THE FUCK is this look?
VIMSY: [*blushing*] Ahh, I have this / interview.
STEKKIE: You sparkling baby / doll!
VIMSY: / Uni interview.

STEKKIE: Interview huh …

VIMSY: Mmhmm. [*Beat*] Gotta go! Enjoy your day!

> VIMSY *bolts for the door.*

STEKKIE: So howzit you affording the Tweety Birds, huh?

VIMSY: [*stopping*] What?

STEKKIE: Using pocket moneys to get your disco biscuits, huh?

VIMSY: Ohmygod no way!

STEKKIE: Comeee now racoon / face.

VIMSY: / RACOON face?!

STEKKIE: I wasn't born yesterday, Vims, and I'ma Joburg girl you can tell me these things.

> VIMSY *turns.*

VIMSY: I don't usually—just this once! Promise me you won't tell Ma? Or Zadie? They'll freak.

STEKKIE: [*grinning*] You want an icicle?

> STEKKIE *pulls an icy pole out of her gown pocket.*

VIMSY: [*eyes widening*] Ohhhhhhhh yeahyeahyeah I want an icy—

> VIMSY *grabs the icy pole. Sucks on it.*

UGH! So good.

> VIMSY *takes* STEKKIE *in.*

[*Sucking*] So Joburg, hey? Big rave scene in Joburg. I mean I haven't been but Resident Advisor they sometimes do articles on DJs popping off in South Africa and—Woooaaaahhhhhh shit son! Would ya check out ttthat tattt!

STEKKIE: Wah?

VIMSY: That tatt your tatt that is that?!

STEKKIE: Oh.

VIMSY: God, my mum would *NEVERRRR* let me have a tatt whatsitof?

STEKKIE: Kudu lily.

VIMSY: Whatsa 'kudy lily'?

STEKKIE: Flower that could kill a man—COME NOW we have things to do!

VIMSY: [*noticing*] Is that my mum's gown?!

STEKKIE: In Yolandi's room, you want a face mask?

VIMSY: Oh, nahnahnahnahnahnahnah Stekkie I have this uni—

STEKKIE: Vimsy please, anyone making you interviewz in this state hasn't got your best interests at heart.

VIMSY: I knowww, but I have to—

STEKKIE: Babydoll, stay home with me, come down with me.

> STEKKIE *saunters over to the home phone.*

VIMSY: But what do I say to—?

STEKKIE: I'll tell THA DEAN you got a fever.

VIMSY: A fever?!

STEKKIE: YAH! That you burning up!

> STEKKIE *smirks, puts the phone to her ear. There's no dial tone.*

Haiboh … This phone broke or what?

VIMSY: Broken?

> VIMSY *walks over, grabs the phone, listens to the dial tone.*

It's fine?

> STEKKIE *shrugs it off.*

STEKKIE: Change of plan Vimsy, time for big girl things, time for YOU to take charge.

VIMSY: Me!?

> STEKKIE *eyes* VIMSY.

> VIMSY *picks up a post-it-note stuck to the phone. It has 'NOTRE DAME CAMPUS' and a phone number written in thick black marker on it.*

> VIMSY *dials the number. Puts on a sick voice.*

[*On the phone*] Um hi there … this is Vimsy, Vimsy Peterson. I'd like to speak to someone from the department of education please. [*Beat*] It's about my interview. At twelve today. I don't think I'll be coming in this arvo.

> STEKKIE *grins.*

I don't think I can.

> *Neon light. Thumping music.*

> STEKKIE *takes* VIMSY *through a rite of passage.*

The following text can be delivered anytime during the sequence.

STEKKIE: When you start living life like you want, they judge you like a hen waiting to get necked. Judging you on the plumpness of your breasts and thickness of your legs and if you standing there all scared ass with a chest full of fear and

thighs trembling

thighs trembling

cos   you   fearing   some   older   bitch   hitting   your CALVESWITHASTICKANDMAKINGTHEM PINK. You won't last, my girl. You won't last anywhere.

STEKKIE *turns to* VIMSY.

How the FUCK you supposed to get anywhere with fear like that?! No-one has my bigness. WHAT I SAY?!

VIMSY: No-one has my bigness.

STEKKIE: Say it again!

VIMSY: No-one has my bigness!

STEKKIE: LOUDER man!

VIMSY: NO-ONE HAS MY BIGNESS!!!

A beat drops.

STEKKIE *and* VIMSY *do a routine of pure black joy.*

They could slide or twerk but whatever they're doing it's spontaneous and fun and for no-one but themselves.

SCENE FIVE

House. That night.

Magic Space. Maybe the entire stage glows.

VIMSY *lays in* STEKKIE*'s lap, getting her hair combed.* STEKKIE *is smoking the last of a joint.*

VIMSY: Owwww!

STEKKIE: [*giggling*] When we all lined up to get our heads of hair in heaven, God gave you two heads of hair instead of one.

VIMSY: Well … tell 'God' he can HAVE ONE OF THEM BACK! Can you give the middle bit a scratch?

STEKKIE: Wenaaaa.

> STEKKIE *scratches into* VIMSY*'s crown.*

VIMSY: Ooooooo yeah, that's it.

> VIMSY *leans into* STEKKIE.

I haven't had this in ages.

STEKKIE: Yolandi doesn't do it no more?

VIMSY: … Nah.

STEKKIE: Your ma used to do this to me. Then I used to do it to Zadie. We lived in one big house back then.

VIMSY: Before we moved, huh?

STEKKIE: Uhuh.

VIMSY: What was it like? The house in Africaaa.

> STEKKIE *ponders.*

STEKKIE: Dusty. There was an old bath with lions' feet. We had our heads rinsed under the tap from time to time … Fruit trees … A man down the road named Rock.

VIMSY: Rock??

> STEKKIE *giggles.*

Was that your boo?!

STEKKIE: Granny, Yolandi and me … eventually Arnie, eventually Zadie and eventually—

VIMSY: Where was I?!

STEKKIE: You were there too, Babydoll—too young to remember the moth balls but … there. By the time your curls came I'd scooted to Joburg.

VIMSY: It's so cool that you did that. Scooted awayyy.

STEKKIE: … Hm …

VIMSY: Why'd you leave?

> STEKKIE *reflects.*

Stekkie?

STEKKIE: There was a fight. Me and the family we … one thing led to another and I had no choice but to flee. [*Beat*] Their hard carping eyes. Looking at me like I was—

> STEKKIE *recoils.*

Shit! I'm high, man.

VIMSY: Whose eyes???

STEKKIE: No-one's.

VIMSY: [*pushing*] Is everything okay with you and Mum?

STEKKIE: [*harshly*] Vimsy! Stop poking your nose!

VIMSY: Okay. Sorry.

> STEKKIE *softens.* STEKKIE *scratches* VIMSY*'s crown.*

> VIMSY *pops up.*

[*Stoned-like*] You know! I don't know where I wanna be! But I know it's not here!

STEKKIE: Well, play your cards right and you might come with me.

VIMSY: Come with you?

STEKKIE: Maybe.

VIMSY: If I could, Stekkieee, I'd rest with you all my life.

STEKKIE: With me?

VIMSY: With you. All the way to Joburg. Jozi. Africaaaa.

> VIMSY *almost lifts into the air at the thought of this.*

ZADIE: What are you doing?

> ZADIE *stands in the doorway wearing scrubs.*

STEKKIE: Cute scrubs, Zadie baby!

VIMSY: Why're you home so late—?

ZADIE: [*to* VIMSY] Late appointment, I finished late. How was your interview?

VIMSY: Interview?

ZADIE: Yeah, how was it?

VIMSY: Uh … good! The interview was—ImetwithNadine.

> ZADIE *furrows her brow.*

ZADIE: Nadine?

VIMSY: Yeah! Nadine, the dean. Nice lady.

STEKKIE: Yah, Nadine the dean, nice lady yah yah.

ZADIE: Right. [*Beat*] What are you guys doing?

> *Notices the glow on their faces.*

Are you two high?

STEKKIE: / Yes.

VIMSY: / No

VIMSY *whacks* STEKKIE. *Stoned giggles.*

ZADIE: Oh my god …

> *A slow beat flows into the room. As if* STEKKIE *has channelled it from her psyche. Something sexy and alien to Paradise.*

STEKKIE: Come onnn Zadie, a bit of dagga never went astray.

> STEKKIE *starts dancing.*

> ZADIE *gets a lil dazed from the atmosphere.*

ZADIE: Woah … the air is pretty th iii cck

STEKKIE: … Dance with me …

> *Something takes over* ZADIE. *She drops her bag and moves in sync with* STEKKIE. *They groove. We're here for a bit.* VIMSY *sits entranced on the floor.*

ZADIE: Where'd you get this weed?

STEKKIE: [*dancing*] The street.

ZADIE: [*dancing*] What do you mean 'the street'?

> STEKKIE *ignores* ZADIE. *Swings her hips.*

> ZADIE *stops.*

Stekkie.

> *Something hits the house. It's loud. The three women turn.*

VIMSY: Wait, was that …?

ZADIE: Sh.

> ZADIE *opens the window. Looks out at the stillness.*

VIMSY: Anybody out there?

ZADIE: —

VIMSY: Zadie?

STEKKIE: Must be that orange throw, no???

VIMSY: [*shivering*] Woaaahhh I've got the freaking / heeeeeebies.

STEKKIE: / Haiii initially I thought this suburb was peaceful man, but I knew, knew as soon as I stepped onto the dark bitumen of Paradise, things were not as they seemed.

> ZADIE *shuts the window.*

> ZADIE *stomps over and turns the music off.*

ZADIE: No more. Okay? Both of you.

STEKKIE: Haiiiboh!

VIMSY: Booooooooooooooo!

ZADIE: [*to* VIMSY] Who are you boo-ing stoner sloth?

VIMSY: I'm not a stoner—!

STEKKIE: Turn the music on, Zadie.

ZADIE: It's time for bed / Stekkie.

VIMSY: / BED?!

STEKKIE: I said turn it on.

> ZADIE *gets a WhatsApp msg from* SHARRON *across the road.*

ZADIE: Fuck!

VIMSY: Who is it?

ZADIE: Sharron. The noise.

VIMSY: UgghGETALIFESharron!

STEKKIE: Who's Sharron?

VIMSY: Tall, weasel looking lady across the road. She hates Mum.

STEKKIE: Why's she hate—?

ZADIE: She doesn't *hate* Mum!

VIMSY: Yes, she does! Mum's coming for her throne.

ZADIE: Mum's not 'coming for her throne', and Sharron's basically our next of kin this summer, stop spreading lies Satan.

STEKKIE: Why'm I not your next of kin?

> ZADIE *looks up at* STEKKIE. *Beat. She ignores* STEKKIE *and goes back to texting.*

Shame you look like shit, Zadie baby.

VIMSY: She's a stress head.

ZADIE: I'm not a stress / head.

STEKKIE: / Bags under your eyes—

ZADIE: I worked all day—

STEKKIE: Hair and out of place—

ZADIE: Drop it.

STEKKIE: Feeling sorry for yourself.

> *Tension.*

[*Pointedly*] Let's go out Vim Tim.

ZADIE: Outside?

STEKKIE: Gonna get this ORANGE TROWA!!
VIMSY: Boo yah!

> VIMSY *runs to her bedroom.*

ZADIE: What do you mean 'get this'—whatareyoutwogonna—?

> STEKKIE *races outside. A whirlwind around* ZADIE.

Wait, Stekkie!

> *A bustling light re-enters. It's* VIMSY *with her phone.*

VIMSY: [*to* ZADIE] Have you seen my Uggs?!
ZADIE: [*to* VIMSY] I threw them out.
VIMSY: [*to* ZADIE] What?!
ZADIE: [*to* VIMSY] They were disgusting.
VIMSY: [*to* ZADIE] It's *my* stuff!
ZADIE: [*to* VIMSY] Well, maybe keep less junk?!
VIMSY: UGHH!

> VIMSY *goes to exit.*

ZADIE: Vims.

> VIMSY *stops.*

Don't. Please.
VIMSY: But—!
ZADIE: This isn't some joke.

> VIMSY *looks towards the door. A fork in the road.*

Seriously.

> VIMSY *concedes. Clicks off her torch.*

VIMSY: Fiiinne.
ZADIE: And go to bed.
VIMSY: I'm goinggg.

> VIMSY *goes to leave.*

STEKKIE: [*from outside*] WHERE ARE YOU ORANGE FUCKER?!

> *The sisters turn.*

ZADIE: Wait is she—?
STEKKIE: [*shouting outside*] SHOW YOURSELF YOU PISS ASS!!

> *Outside, a car alarm goes off.*

ZADIE *turns white.*

ZADIE: Oh my god …

    Blackout.

SCENE SIX

The next morning. Wednesday.

House.

SHARRON *is sitting opposite* ZADIE. ZADIE*'s hair is in a pineapple.*

SHARRON: Firstly, my son Caiden was trying to sleep when he heard music and things.

ZADIE: Right.

SHARRON: Then my hubby came out and *he* heard alarms and yelling and things.

ZADIE: Okay.

SHARRON: Everything was rattling, Zadie. By no means do I usually have an issue with music but … big booming drums, you know? And expletive language, you know?

ZADIE: I understand, Sharron. I'm so sorry! We had a guest. Someone … unexpected and things got out of hand, but I completely understand how disrespectful that must of / seemed.

SHARRON: / Okay.

ZADIE: It won't happen again!

SHARRON: Good. Look, we didn't make a noise complaint to the police last night—

ZADIE: The police?!

SHARRON: Yes. Everyone heard. Number 37 right through to 77, everyone on the WhatsApp group.

ZADIE: Oh …

SHARRON: And your Mum—*Yolaandi*—weknoweachotherfromthe Paradise§ and—

ZADIE: Please don't tell Yolandi.

    SHARRON*'s eyes widen.*

SHARRON: Well, *she* informed me before she jetted off that she would like to run for president this year …

ZADIE: [*beaming*] Yes!

SHARRON: For the first time ever!

ZADIE: She's really passionate about it!

SHARRON: I should let you know that at the committee, keeping things calm and quiet in Paradise *is* our ethos. So, we'd hate for this … disruption to affect Yolandi's prospects.

ZADIE: Of course. I'd hate for that to happen.

SHARRON: Wouldbeashame.

> *Beat.*

ZADIE: I'll make sure we keep it down! And I'm sorry for waking up your son.

SHARRON: Caiden's got these big fat tonsils so he's a very light sleeper.

ZADIE: Right.

SHARRON: Mouth breather.

ZADIE: Right.

SHARRON: They're always inflamed.

ZADIE: That sucks.

SHARRON: Constant tonsillitis.

ZADIE: Have you thought about getting them removed?

SHARRON: Operations aren't Caiden's thing.

> *Beat.*

ZADIE: Hey Sharron, it's great you're here because there's something I'd love to run by you.

SHARRON: Something by me?

> ZADIE *braces herself.*

ZADIE: An incident. We found something, on our house, this week. We think there may be some sort of … vandalism occruring in the area.

> *Beat.*

SHARRON: Vandalism?

ZADIE: Vandalism. It's gonna sound silly but someone's been throwing stuff. At night. At us. Like *whack!* onto the brick.

SHARRON: I'm not really sure what you're insinuating, pet?

ZADIE: No! I'm not insinuating anything! I guess I'm just bringing it up because … you haven't seen or heard of anything strange happening in the area, have you?

SHARRON: What about the other young lady that lives here? Does she know anything?

ZADIE: No. Unfortunately, we're both are pretty stumped.

SHARRON: There's never been any vandalism in this area. Not in Paradise.

ZADIE: … No.

SHARRON: And the only thing's been strange has been the noise and yelling and things coming from your house.

ZADIE: Yeah …

SHARRON: My husband hasn't mentioned anything. Paul. And he's in charge of crime control over at the committee and he's usually across these things.

ZADIE: Dad's told me about Paul's posters!

SHARRON: Your dad?

ZADIE: Yeah! Arnie?

SHARRON: Oohhh, *Mr RnB.*

ZADIE: Hm?

SHARRON: We've never really caught conversation, but he used to play this … RnB, *very loudly* when he washed his car.

ZADIE: Oh, I remember he used to do that. So embarrassing.

SHARRON: Paul had a little word to him. So, when are they back exactly? *Mr Rnb* and your mum?

ZADIE: In a week—so do you think it's worth calling the cops? About the vandalism?

SHARRON: Depends. A policeman might not take you seriously, might think it's a prank or something, given the good track record of this area.

ZADIE: That's … exactly why I'm reluctant.

SHARRON *spots something.*

SHARRON: Pardon me, whose knickers are they?

ZADIE: Knickers?

SHARRON *points to a bright pink G-string on the floor.*

Oh. My sister's.

SHARRON: Should be in the laundry, no?

ZADIE: Yep! Laundry.

ZADIE *chucks the G-string out of sight.*

SHARRON *spots her watch.*

SHARRON: Ooo! I should head off, I have Zumba at eleven. Look, all-in-all, we just don't want any unsavoury behaviour in the area.

ZADIE: Yes! Absolutely! Thanks so much, Sharron!

SHARRON: Thank *you* so much, Zadie! Such a gorgeous name by the way, like the cleaning lady.

ZADIE: Sorry?

SHARRON: Oh, you know? Farnsie!

[*Singing*] Ahhh Sadie, the cleaning lady! With a trusty scrubbing brush and pail of water—Aussie classic.

ZADIE *attempts to sing along.*

[*Singing*] / Ahhh Sadie, the cleaning lady!

ZADIE: [*singing*] / Ahhh Sadie, the cleaning lady!

SHARRON: That's it!

ZADIE: It's really nice to finally meet you, Sharron! I'm sure Mum would love to have a cuppa when / she's back.

SHARRON: / You're very pretty by the way. Such gorgeous hair.

ZADIE: Thank you.

ZADIE *tucks her hair.*

SHARRON: It must be hard to brush.

ZADIE: It can be, yours would be much easier.

SHARRON: Oh, this old rag?

SHARRON *touches her wig.*

ZADIE: [*admiringly*] Honestly, it's so smooth, like a … Pantene ad.

SHARRON: Does yours get knotty?

ZADIE: Ugh all the time if I leave it—

SHARRON: If I had hair like yours my hubby would get a pair of garden secateurs and go:

SHARRON *mimes secateurs.*

Whew! Whew! Whew!

SHARRON *giggles.* ZADIE *giggles.*

/ Hehehehehehehehahahahahahahahahahahahahahahahahahah.

ZADIE: / Hehehehehehehehahahahahahahahahahahahahah.

SHARRON: Anyway, appreciate this chat, Sadie.

SHARRON *tottles off.*

ZADIE *stands alone.*

STEKKIE: Baby doll.

ZADIE *startles. She sees* STEKKIE, *wearing* YOLANDI*'s hat, bathers, and sunnies.*

ZADIE: Stekkie … Hi.

STEKKIE: Who was here just now?

ZADIE: Um, no-one. Postman.

STEKKIE *saunters through, singing to herself.*

STEKKIE: [*singing*] Postman Pat, Postman Pat, Postman Pat and his black and white cat.

Tell me, how's my hair looking? Does it look nice? I'm bout to bake outside and I want to make sure— [*Spotting her G-string*] My G-string!

STEKKIE *snatches the pink thong.*

Been looking for this.

ZADIE: Hey Stekkie, can we talk?

Beat.

STEKKIE: Talk? Why talk?

ZADIE: Just for a sec.

STEKKIE *sits.* ZADIE *sits.*

Last night. You … shouting. Like that. Outside. You can't—

STEKKIE: I told you Zadie, that alarm went off by itself. I didn't touch the car.

ZADIE: You can't behave like that. Okay? You just can't.

Beat.

STEKKIE: Like what?

ZADIE: Like … how you do. Not here.

STEKKIE: And … how do I do?

ZADIE: [*firmly*] You know what I mean.

Mum and Dad have sacrificed a lot. We used to live in a pretty bad area, Stekkie. When we got here, from S.A., they saved and scrambled and put away and now they own this house. You know what that means, don't you? I mean, you've never—

They came here with nothing—and now we are … better, so it's up to you to behave, okay?

STEKKIE *lours.*

STEKKIE: Tell me, what do you constitute as good behaviour, Zadie? Shaming me? Is that good behaviour in your books? [*Scoffs*] My my my. Just like your mother, huh?

ZADIE: Stekkie. I know you and Ma have things you—but her and I are completely different.

STEKKIE *'s voice turns to ice.*

STEKKIE: Different? You telling me, you don't see me how she sees me? I don't think you and her are different, my child. I think you two are exactlyyy the same. [*Whispering*] Exactlyexactlyexactly.

A lump grows in ZADIE *'s throat. A darkness creeps into the room.*

ZADIE: Listen, I'm just trying to—

STEKKIE: [*hissing*] Thiss fucking family, y'all trying to get rid of me, again?

ZADIE *'s body vibrates.*

Her arm lifts, her fingers pull into the shape of a gun. She points it directly at STEKKIE *'s head.*

STEKKIE *'s face loses its life.*

What's this? Zadie? [*Beat*] That. I'm telling you. That's not child's play, Zadie. That's not …

An unravelling across ZADIE *'s face. She lets go of the gun. Looks down at her hand. Then back at* STEKKIE. *Then back at her hand.*

ZADIE: I don't know why I—

STEKKIE: You gonna pull that thing on me?

ZADIE: I didn't know it would—

STEKKIE: That's how you gonna get rid of me?

ZADIE: —

STEKKIE: [*spitting*] Footsack man.

ZADIE: Wait, what have I …?

STEKKIE *storms off.*

Stekkie??? What have I done????????????????????????

A tiny 'thmp' against the window.

LEROY: LIMUN TROWAAAAAAAAAAAA—

> LEROY *pops his head up, races into the house. He's holding a lemon and strikes a pose.*

AHAHAHAHAHAHAAHAHAHAAHH …

> LEROY *stops. Notices* ZADIE.

Get it? 'Limun trowa' cos of the … oranges.

ZADIE: Yep.

LEROY: I was in the garden bed. Hiding. Thinking you'd … comeout. You alright, Z?

> *And in a disturbingly efficient way,* ZADIE *squashes it all down. Regains herself.*

ZADIE: Yep, I'm fine.

LEROY: You went pretty dark there for a second?

ZADIE: Nah! I was just—silly!

LEROY: Ain't silly. We said one-thirty right?

ZADIE: One-thirty?

> LEROY *gives a coy smile.*

LEROY: Hoyts. Did you forget?

ZADIE: [*realising*] Ohhhh shit—

LEROY: Ahhhh shiiit—

ZADIE: Leroyyy! I completely forgot, dude!

LEROY: Don't sweat it … *dude!*

ZADIE: The movies and everything. I'm sorry, it's been such a huge week. Those oranges, they've been hitting the house and—

LEROY: Again?

> LEROY *looks to the window.*

> ZADIE *nods.*

Far out … [*Beat*] Hey, we don't have to see *Tenet* this arvo.

> LEROY *walks up to* ZADIE.

Why don't we have a stake-out?

ZADIE: A stake-out?

LEROY: Yeah. Tonight. Catch the fool doing this shit.

ZADIE: I don't knoww—

LEROY: We could do it on the roof?

ZADIE: The roof?!

LEROY: You and me? Up there. Over Paradise.

> LEROY *touches her wrist lightly.*

We can figure this out. I'm here for you, you know? Minus the flip-flops.

> LEROY *grins.*

ZADIE: Just *promise me* we'll be quiet, and quick. And when nothing happens, we'll come climb back down?

LEROY: We'll be quiet and quick and climb back down.

SCENE SEVEN

That night.

The roof.

VIMSY *sits awkwardly between* LEROY *and* ZADIE. VIMSY *has binoculars and a torch.*

They're looking up at the stars.

VIMSY: If you look closely you can see the shaft—

LEROY: Where's the shaft?

VIMSY: There! And those two circles make up the ball sack.

LEROY: Where? Down the bottom?

VIMSY: *Under* the shaft.

LEROY: Nah that's a pretty skinny shaft yo.

VIMSY: Oooooo. [*Imitating him*] 'That's a pretty skinny shaft yo.' Not thick like L Daddy's shaft.

ZADIE: [*big man voice*] L Daddy has a big boy shaft.

VIMSY: Not a little skinny star boy shaft!

> VIMSY *cackles.*

ZADIE: Ssshhh! You'll wake someone up.

> *They look over Paradise.*

What time is it?

LEROY: Nearly nine.

ZADIE: Should we go back down? It's getting late.

VIMSY: Nah mate it ain't late, this is prime time.

ZADIE: [*scoffing*] Prime time?

VIMSY: [*looking through binoculars*] Plus, I got my eye on Shaz and Paul.

LEROY: Who's Sharron and—?

ZADIE: Don'tt be ridiculous.

VIMSY: Don't defend these people, Zadie. It's either *her* or Caiden.

ZADIE: Caiden?!

LEROY: You think it's them, Vims?

VIMSY: [*through binoculars*] Mmhm.

    Beat.

LEROY: Oi. Five-year-plan.

ZADIE: What?

LEROY: I wanna know your five-year-goals!

ZADIE: Why?

LEROY: Go on Zadie.

ZADIE: Uh okay … um … a big house.

LEROY: A big house?

ZADIE: Yep! My own. I'd own my own big ole house. And it'll have large windows. And stone floors! And minimalist architecture! And Aesop handwash!

VIMSY: [*under her breath*] Sometimes I swear you're a white girl.

ZADIE: And a bidet!

LEROY: What's a bidet?

VIMSY: Thing that squirts water up your butt.

LEROY: Where would the house be?

ZADIE: I don't know … I've never been anywhere.

VIMSY: Uh uh South Africa. What about there?!

    ZADIE *doesn't respond.*

LEROY: What about you, Vims?

VIMSY: Ooooo, I don't know *really* but I'm starting to think … maybe that's chill!

ZADIE: What do you mean 'maybe that's / chill'?

VIMSY: / I don't think I want a degree.

ZADIE *eyes* VIMSY.

Yep! I've decided that I'm in a state of indecision. Instead, I'm gonna focus on the important things. Be a PROUDDD coloured girl, move to a fast city like Sydney or Joburg, learn how to DJ, listen to techno and start my own record label. Something like that. Somethin like Stekkie, you know?

And have a girlfriend with a high IQ! And a big butt!

ZADIE: You can't work at Chook Treat your whole life?

VIMSY: I mean I love it so … maybe I can.

Beat.

ZADIE: Vims, have you been going to Martin's bush doofs?

VIMSY: … Why does it matter?

ZADIE: [*to* LEROY] Leroy, has Vims been going to Martin bush doofs—?

LEROY: Um, I dunno if I should—

VIMSY: What's the big deal???

ZADIE: No big deal Vims. It's just great to hear that you went to a party the night before your interview.

VIMSY: To be honest, I didn't go to my interview so it doesn't matter.

Beat.

ZADIE: … What?

VIMSY: Yep. I didn't go.

ZADIE: You didn't go???

VIMSY: I'm in flux!

Awkward beat. ZADIE *seethes.*

LEROY: Yo, for what it's worth Vizz Fizz, those are some good priorities you got.

VIMSY: Thanks Li Li. [*Beat*] Would you still be doing that swimming ting?

LEROY: Yeah! And I want to own my own lap pool. Mainly so I don't have to catch two buses to train every day, buttt I guess that would take money so a bit of money would be rad.

He looks up at the night sky.

And I want to be closer to God.

ZADIE: What do you mean?

LEROY: I feel like in five years' time I'll know. Figure out how to be closer to the big boy upstairs.

LEROY *looks down at his crucifix.*

Not just have some gold around my neck.

ZADIE *scoffs.*

[*To* ZADIE] What?

ZADIE: … Nothing.

LEROY: Why'd you scoff?

ZADIE: That just doesn't seem like a *tangible* thing.

LEROY: What do you mean?

ZADIE: How do you even measure that?

LEROY: I don't know, Zadie, it doesn't need to be 'measured'.

ZADIE: It just doesn't seem like a realistic goal. It might not happen and then what?

LEROY: No Zadie! It *will* happen and when it does, I'll feel closer to myself—maybe not when I'm twenty-seven but at some point, okay?

ZADIE: Okay! Shit.

Beat.

LEROY: [*under his breath*] Fuck this.

LEROY *gets up.*

ZADIE: What???

LEROY: I'm out.

ZADIE: Leroy! / Chill!

VIMSY: [*getting up*] / Maybee I should give y'all some space.

ZADIE: Vims, no!

VIMSY: Zadie.

VIMSY *stands her ground.*

You two hash this out.

VIMSY *moves off.*

She leaves ZADIE *and* LEROY *to hash it out.*

As we transition: An echo of voices envelop the house.

They sing the Zulu lullaby 'Thula Thula': Thula thul, thula baba, thula sana, Tul'ubab 'uzobuya ekuseni.

The voices loop into a haunting.

Then ...

SCENE EIGHT

A home phone rings. It rings and rings.

Down in the house. That same night.

An answering machine.

YOLANDI: [*voiceover, from machine*] Hi there, you've reached the Peterson household of Yolandi,

ARNIE: [*voiceover, from machine*] Arnie,

VIMSY: [*voiceover, from machine*] Vimsy!

ZADIE: [*voiceover, from machine*] And Zadie.

YOLANDI: [*voiceover, from machine*] We're not at home right now but leave us a message and we'll call you back as quick as we can!

YOLANDI's tired voice from the machine.

Hi. It's Mumma. Was just calling to say hi. And that we've had some news.

A silhouette appears.

We've had some sad news, bubba. Some tragic stuff here in S.A. Hm.

The silhouette comes forward. It's STEKKIE.

Your cousin, Zadie. I'm sure you remember her ...?

STEKKIE listens.

She's passed on. No longer with us.

STEKKIE's hand hovers over the phone.

Shame. She was a lost cause, man.

STEKKIE clenches her fist.

My child, it looks like we'll be here a little longer. You must give us a call back when you can, okay? Hope everything's okay. Love you. Bubye.

STEKKIE's face comes up to us. Then down to the machine. Then she presses delete.

A stretch of silence.

VIMSY: Stekkie.

STEKKIE: [*startled*] Oh. Hi Babydoll.

VIMSY *sulks in.* STEKKIE *wipes her face.*

What's up?

VIMSY: Eh. Zadie's being a bitch.

STEKKIE: Is she now? Why? What's she doing?

Beat.

VIMSY *looks at* STEKKIE *with big eyes.*

VIMSY: When are you going back to S.A., Stekkie?

STEKKIE *hardens.*

STEKKIE: S.A. Why you asking me about S.A.?

VIMSY: I was thinking, Stekkie, for ages now I've been thinking maybe I should come with you? To Africa. I haven't been since I was little but maybe I could—?

STEKKIE: Come with me?

VIMSY: Yeah … I don't have much here,

STEKKIE: Yes, you do.

VIMSY: Just like Chook Treat and stuff but I can sort that.

STEKKIE: Nonono there's nothing to sort. Stop this now Vimsy, you're being a baby.

Beat.

VIMSY: … I'm not being a baby.

STEKKIE: You are.

VIMSY: But I thought—?

STEKKIE: What you thought? That you'd be my bundle? That's what babies do Vimsy, they *rely* on others.

This crushes VIMSY.

Now get up there, stop being a lost cause and grow up.

VIMSY *turns to leave.*

Then stops.

VIMSY: Hey, is everything alright?

STEKKIE: Leave me now.

VIMSY: Did something—?

> STEKKIE *turns her back.*
>
> *A sore* VIMSY *exits back onto the roof.*
>
> *Pause.*
>
> *Grief grabs hold of* STEKKIE. *She looks down into the phone. Then to the door. And leaves.*

SCENE NINE

The roof.

The same quiet night.

LEROY *is standing sulking into the night.* ZADIE *is sitting awkwardly.*

ZADIE: Sorry. I didn't mean to … make you feel dumb. Sorry.

> LEROY *turns. She grins at him.*

I guess we're even after that lemon prank?
LEROY: … I guess.

> LEROY *smiles. He sits down next to her.*

What do you think your sister's doing?
ZADIE: Probably.playing.The Sims.

> *Tension.*
>
> *The pair suddenly lunge at each other. But instead of kissing they bang foreheads.*

LEROY: Ooooooooooooo / ooooo
ZADIE: / Owwwww shit!
> [*Holding her head*] Sorry, sorrrryyy.
LEROY: [*holding his head*] It's chill.

> *They try again. Clang teeth.*

ZADIE: Watchwatch the teeth.
LEROY: Oh yep.

> *Finally, they successfully pash! It's fumbly but they're soooo into it.*
>
> ZADIE *arches her back into it. She goes for an ambitious crotch grab. But aims little low.*

[*Whispering*] Ey! Careful, careful.

ZADIE: Oh fuck! Did I—?

LEROY: *Jussssstttt*, my balls.

ZADIE: Did I squish / them?

LEROY: / Yep yip.

>   LEROY *fixes himself.*

ZADIE: Shit! Sorry! I'm so dumb, I don't know why I—

LEROY: Nah, it'sallgood, tis allllgooooood.

>   ZADIE *goes for another kiss.*

Justonesec.

>   LEROY *inhales. Exhales.*

Hnng.

ZADIE: You okay?

LEROY: Mmhm.

>   *They sit. Agony.*

>   *Finally,* VIMSY *climbs back up.*

VIMSY: You guys good?

ZADIE: Yerrrp.

>   VIMSY *plonks herself down.*

What's Stekkie doing?

VIMSY: Um I don't know, she's being … weird.

ZADIE: What do you mean 'weird'?

VIMSY: [*suspiciously*] Have you spoken to her today?

ZADIE: Not really. Why? What's up?

VIMSY: No reason.

>   *Beat.*

You two sort your shit out?

ZADIE: Mhm.

>   LEROY *gets up.*

Whereareyougoing?!

LEROY: Gonna go climb, look fo clues.

VIMSY: Can I come?

ZADIE: Vims, stay here.

VIMSY: But I wanna climb—

ZADIE: Stay!

> VIMSY *huffs. Complies with* ZADIE.

> LEROY *climbs away.*

VIMSY: You shouldn't patronise him like that.

ZADIE: I didn't patronise him?

VIMSY: Religion is his thing, Zadie. He's trying to figure out.

ZADIE: All I said was—

VIMSY: It'sa bit rich, you piping up about it. You used to do the sign of the cross when you were nervous.

ZADIE: That was irony?

VIMSY: Sure.

> *Beat.*

> ZADIE *looks out at Leroy. Climbing fences towards* SHARRON*'s house.*

ZADIE: I don't know if I want to end up with a Catholic boy anyway.

VIMSY: Oh come onnn he's not *that* Catholic—

ZADIE: Could you imagine? Yuck.

VIMSY: He doesn't even go to church!

ZADIE: Doesn't he?

VIMSY: That's what Martin said.

> ZADIE *death stares* VIMSY.

ZADIE: We should go back inside.

VIMSY: What are you afraid of?

ZADIE: Nothing. I'm just tired and can't be bothered having this conversation.

VIMSY: You're always tired.

ZADIE: Yes Vims, because some of us have to work.

VIMSY: I *work*???

ZADIE: Asking people what flavour basting they want on their chicken isn't work.

> *This stings.*

VIMSY: …You're very curt when you're tired.

> ZADIE *grabs the binoculars and looks out at Leroy.*

ZADIE: [*under her breath*] Far out, Leroy.

> VIMSY *looks out.*

VIMSY: What's he up to? [*Spotting Leroy*] Is he climbing their fence? He'll never make that, it's huge and there's nothing to grab onto—

> *A thump noise.*

How did he do that?

ZADIE: [*panicking*] He's gonna wake someone up.

VIMSY: It's finee—

ZADIE: He just climbed their fence!

VIMSY: Whose fence?

ZADIE: Sharron's fence! Someone's gonna catch him.

VIMSY: Yo have a little bit of faith.

> *They watch. A light turns on.*

ZADIE: Oh my / god.

VIMSY: Wait, did a light just switch / on?

ZADIE: / Oh my god—

VIMSY: Who's out there?

ZADIE: I don't know!

VIMSY: Who's that?

ZADIE: Some man. He's on the back patio.

VIMSY: Is it Sharron's husband?

ZADIE: Idon'tknow! I guess so. Must be Paul?

VIMSY: Where's Leroy?

ZADIE: There!

VIMSY: Where?

ZADIE: On the roof!

VIMSY: Which roof?!

ZADIE: SHARRON'S SHED ROOF!

> *They wait impatiently.*

VIMSY: [*whispering*] Get tha heck outta there, man.

> *A louder thump noise.*

ZADIE: OH MY GOD.

VIMSY: Whatjusthappened?

ZADIE: OHH MY/ GOD!

VIMSY: / Is he okay?

ZADIE: No, he's not okay!

VIMSY: DID HE JUST FALL?!

ZADIE: Yeshejustfell! Grab the torch!

VIMSY: What do I do??!!

ZADIE: Distract them! Quick! Flash the light onto the house or something!

> VIMSY *grabs the torch.*

But don't shine it onto the man's faCe—

> VIMSY *flashes the light but accidently shines Paul in the face. Paul notices them.*
>
> *Both girls freak and duck.*

VIMS!

VIMSY: Holy shit!!

ZADIE: I said *not* onto his face!

VIMSY: It was an accident! Did he see us?!

ZADIE: I don't know!

VIMSY: Have I stuffed it? What do we do?!

ZADIE: We gotta get down!

VIMSY: What?!

ZADIE: WegottagetTHE FUCKdown! Now!

VIMSY: THIS IS COOKED!!

ZADIE: Freaking move!

> ZADIE *and* VIMSY *crab along the roof.*

SCENE TEN

The same quiet night.

The neighbours' back patio.

PAUL *stands facing out.*

It's a hot night, so naturally he's wearing shorts.

PAUL: [*to himself*] Christ on a bike.

> SHARRON *enters tying up her nightgown.*

SHARRON: Who's out there, Paul? Paul. Who's out there? Did you see anyone?

PAUL: Go back inside, Sharron.

SHARRON: Who was it?

Beat.

Gosh. On the shed? [*Beat*] Oh Paul—

PAUL: Go back inside, Sharron.

SHARRON: Did he touch any of my washing?

PAUL: Inside, Sharron.

SHARRON *goes to exit. Stops, turns.*

SHARRON: But what about my washing?

PAUL: Sharron—

SHARRON: Did he steal any of my whites?

PAUL: I don't think so.

SHARRON: My good whites?

PAUL: I think it's best if you—

SHARRON: Get his grubby hands all over them?

PAUL: Go back inside.

SHARRON: Hands covered in godknowswhat all over my—

PAUL: Sharron—

SHARRON: Not what you want on your Wednesday night, is it?

PAUL: In-side. Go back. Sharron inside.

Another thump noise. PAUL *and* SHARRON *scream.*

SHARRON: Golly!

PAUL: [*pointing*] THERE HE IS!

SHARRON: There he is Paul!—In the hoodie!—On the fence!

LEROY *disappears. They stop.*

PAUL: Where's-hee-gorn?

They wait.

Smashing glass.

The house alarm goes off.

SHARRON *and* PAUL *freak.*

SHARRON: What was that?!

PAUL *checks inside.*

PAUL: The house Shaz! He's in the house! He's gone through the bloody skylight!!

SHARRON: Caiden's SKY LIGHT??!!

Suddenly a light is shone onto PAUL*'s face. It's huge and blinding and ancestral.*

PAUL *grimaces and topples over.*

PAUL: AAAHH!!

PAUL *might grab onto* SHARRON*'s nightgown when he loses his balance.*

SHARRON: PAUL! MY SHAWL!!!

PAUL*'s ball sack might flop out of his shorts.* SHARRON*'s tit might flash. Total fuckery.*

PAUL: What was that?!

PAUL *retreats away from the light.*

SHARRON: A light of sorts!! Where did it come from, Paul?

PAUL: Across the road.

SHARRON: [*seething*] *Yolaandi's* girls?

PAUL: Those kids.

SHARRON: Sadie and that frizzy one!

PAUL: Rightrightrightrightriiiiiight in me *FUCKIN RETINAS*! They must be in cahoots with him!

SHARRON: Where's he now, Paul? He's not in the house?!

PAUL *patrols the patio. Sweaty and turbo.*

PAUL: Nahnahnahnahnahnahnah he shot off I think. Usain Bolted it across the front yard.

SHARRON: WHY THE FUCK DIDN'T YOU THINK TO RUN AFTER HIM PAUL?!

PAUL: Well of course I did Sharron! Of course, I did *THINK* to do that but my knees aren't what they used to be!

SHARRON: First a man up on our shed and now flashing lights and things all over the street like a flipping disco!

A grown man pokes his head out.

CAIDEN: [*crying*] MUM??!!

PAUL: CAIDEN!!! CAIDDDENNNN!!!

PAUL *bolts off to check on* CAIDEN.

SHARRON: I'm calling zero zero zero.

SHARRON *pulls her phone out. She yells across the road.*

I'M CALLING THE COPS!!

SHARRON *dials 000.*

[*On the phone*] Hello? Hello? Police please! This is Sharron, Sharron Youren. No, Youren. YOU-RIN—We run the committee in Paradise over at the Paradise Town Hall—I'm calling cos there's a man causing a threat, a black man in Paradise, currently causing a threat.

SCENE ELEVEN

That night. Same time.

A street in Paradise.

STEKKIE *walks along. Her face wet.*

STEKKIE: [*to herself*] Pull it together, Stukkie. You got this. It's okay. It'll all be okay ...

STEKKIE *stops.*

She looks down the road. Stillness. Suburbia.

She wipes herself clean.

Beat.

The Paradise sky above us cracks open.

A light overcomes STEKKIE.

It's huge and radiant and blinding.

Haiboh.

The unearthly tones of 'Thula Thula' are heard.

They wash over STEKKIE.

An ancestral calming occurs.

She closes her eyes. Peace. Tranquillity.

… I'm listening …

SCENE TWELVE

House. It's dark. A little later.

ZADIE *enters panicked. She peeps through the window. Then ducks. Waits …*

ZADIE *puts her hand to her chest. Does the sign of the cross.*

VIMSY *busts in.*

VIMSY: Dude!

ZADIE: What just happened?

VIMSY: Dudeee!

ZADIE: Where's Leroy???

> VIMSY *peeps through the window.*

[*Whispering*] Duck down!

VIMSY: [*whispering*] Where?

ZADIE: [*whispering*] There!

VIMSY: [*whispering*] Wheretheheck is 'there'?

> VIMSY *ducks.*

Leroy still out there …?

ZADIE: I thought he was behind you?

VIMSY: I thought he was behind *you*! [*Beat*] We gotta go find him.

> VIMSY *gets up.* ZADIE *grabs her arm.*

ZADIE: Don't.

VIMSY: But we can't just leave him?

> LEROY *races in. He's bleeding—a gash on his head.*

Leroy!

> LEROY *ducks.*

ZADIE: What just happened???

LEROY: Holy shit!

ZADIE: What were you doinggg?!?!

LEROY: Holy shit!!

VIMSY: Dude, you're bleeding!

LEROY *touches his head. Does the sign of the cross.*

ZADIE: When did we decide we were gonna break into other people's houses?!

LEROY: I gotta go!

LEROY *gets up. Stops. Grimaces. Holding his arm.*

Hnnnnngggggg.

VIMSY: What's wrong? Are you okay?

LEROY: I fell. My arm. I think I stuffed it—

VIMSY: Really?!

VIMSY *rushes over to him.*

It's okay, just breathe.

LEROY: Ow oww!!

ZADIE *watches them.*

VIMSY: [*to* ZADIE] What do we do? Do we need ice?

VIMSY *runs to get ice.* ZADIE *stands and watches him.*

ZADIE: This isn't a joke, Leroy.

LEROY: Zadie, my arm is cooked so *clearly* I don't think this is a joke.

ZADIE: What were you doing on Sunday?

LEROY: What?

ZADIE: Sunday, where were you?

LEROY: I don't know I had church???

ZADIE: Church? Really?

VIMSY *re-enters with an ice pack.*

Is it you?

LEROY: What?

ZADIE: Have you been throwing them?

VIMSY: Zadie, what the hell?

ZADIE: You threw that lemon.

LEROY: That was a prank!

ZADIE: Stekkie said someone was hanging around the house, someone in boardshorts and *you* said that you go to church on Sundays but you *also* said that you do some 'crazy shit' to get a girl's attention.

And this whole time you've been making these jokes, Leroy—so has it been you? This entire time??? [*Beat*] Sunday night the first orange hit so was that you trying to get my attention? Because if it was that's a pretty fucked up way of getting me to fall in love with you Leroy, that's pretty fucked up if it's been you this entire time!

Beat.

LEROY: Are you serious? You think …?

ZADIE *glares at him.*

You're serious. I feel big things for you Zadie and now you think—?

Sirens from afar.

I gotta go.

VIMSY: But where are you / gonna?

LEROY: / I'm out.

VIMSY: Leroy! You can't just—

LEROY: I gotta get the fuck out of here!

VIMSY: But the cops! And your arm??!! You need ice—

LEROY *leaves.*

LEROY!

Pause.

ZADIE *puts her head into her hands.*

ZADIE: *FFFFUUUUCCCKKKKKK.*

VIMSY: I can't believe you.

ZADIE: It's better if he goes home.

VIMSY: What's wrong with you?

ZADIE: *He* was one who decided to PARKOR his way across Paradise Street so he can just go home and take care of it.

VIMSY: He's hurt himself?!

ZADIE: The cops have been called, Vims.

VIMSY: I know, Zadie—

ZADIE: The literal police are on their way.

VIMSY: Exactly! And you sent him outside? By himself? Also FUCK THE COPS, Zadie! ACAB!

ZADIE: You don't know what you're talking about.

VIMSY: *I* don't know what I'm talking about?

ZADIE: You don't get to tell me how it is, Vims. You're a baby.

VIMSY: What the fuck?!

ZADIE: You work in a chicken shop. And again, thanks for *casually* mentioning that you're not going to be doing anything with your life, Mum's gonna loveeee that.

VIMSY: Hereee we go—

ZADIE: What are you even doing this summer?

VIMSY: You were the one getting fingered in front of everyone!

Beat.

ZADIE: … What?

VIMSY: On the roof. I saw you.

ZADIE: Don't you dare, okay? Don't you DARE say that about me again!

VIMSY: THEN DON'T *DO WHAT YOU DO!*

ZADIE: WHAT DO I DO?!

VIMSY: BE AN UPTIGHT AWFUL BITCH!!

ZADIE *storms up to* VIMSY *and goes to slap her.*

STEKKIE *busts in. There's colour in her face and a twinkle in her eye.*

STEKKIE: Hello my beautiful angels!

STEKKIE *notices them. Stops.*

What's wrong??? Why you so pale in the face?

VIMSY: Stekkie—

ZADIE: Vims.

STEKKIE: Y'all been fighting?

VIMSY: They've called the cops on us. Across the road, the people across the road they—

STEKKIE: They called the cops on you?

VIMSY: Leroy. He fell. Our friend fell down and hurt himself and they—screamed and freaked and now the cops are coming, Stekkie. And Leroy's out there—

STEKKIE: They called the cops on you cos you playing? Just cos you playing outside? [*With contempt*] This is some kak.

ZADIE: Stekkie. I need you to stay here.

STEKKIE: I'll sort them out.

VIMSY: Zadie, Stekkie can talk to Sharron!

ZADIE: No! You both need to promise me you'll—

STEKKIE: I'll talk to Sharron!

ZADIE: You'll be going to your room, getting into bed, pulling the covers the *FUCK* over your head and falling to sleep.

STEKKIE: Why you talking to me like that?

> ZADIE *pulls her fingers into the shape of a gun. She points the gun at* STEKKIE*'s head.*

VIMSY: Wait, what are you—

STEKKIE: Zadie.

ZADIE: [*to* STEKKIE] Why are you here?

STEKKIE: Zadie.

ZADIE: Why *really*? What do you WANT from us?!

> STEKKIE *doesn't answer.*

You are ruining everything for me, everything Mum and Dad have worked for and taught me about how to … be, everything *I've* worked for. If this is you, throwing this SHIT at us every night I want you gone out out of our lives and I want it to stop!

Do you hear me?! I want you and … *IT* OUT!!

> STEKKIE *looks at* ZADIE *with clarity.*

STEKKIE: Zadie. I see a festering—

ZADIE: Don't.

STEKKIE: And on the street tonight I was ready to leave here. But then there were these tones, Zadie—

ZADIE: Stop it.

STEKKIE: These ancestral tones—they came and spoke to me, turned me around and brought me back to you to … help. Because I can see now that we are just pieces of a damaged, bitter ecosystem but we are not to blame, okay? None of us. I left for Joburg all those years ago and I lost my baby—

ZADIE: You can't be here anymore.

STEKKIE: But you two are like my babies.

ZADIE: You don't belong here.

VIMSY: Zadie, please!—

STEKKIE: Y'all are my hearts!

ZADIE: A stupid coloured Stukkie who spits and fucks and drinks.

Pause.

STEKKIE *breaks.*

STEKKIE: Why you pointing that gun at me, Zadie? Why you pointing it at me like I'm dirt on the floor?

VIMSY: Stekkie, she doesn't—

STEKKIE: No, no.

VIMSY: She didn't mean it!

STEKKIE: [*to* VIMSY] Bye now Baby doll.

VIMSY: STEKKIE NO!

STEKKIE: [*to* VIMSY] You don't need me no more.

VIMSY: We do! I do!

STEKKIE: I'm going to go someplace else now, okay? But think of me sometime? [*To herself*] Mustn't feel sorry for myself.

STEKKIE *turns to* ZADIE.

Zadie. No-one has your bigness.

ZADIE *pulls the trigger.*

She shoots STEKKIE *in the head.*

STEKKIE *begins to turn to light.*

Silence.

ZADIE *releases the gun from her hand.*

VIMSY: What have you done?

ZADIE: You don't understand.

VIMSY: I wish people would stop saying 'you don't understand'. I understand. More than you think. [*Beat*] You hate yourself. You look down on who we are cos you feel something *fucking foul* towards yourself. And now Stekkie … who was the best thing to ever happen to us is gone. Gone. Because you can't stand being black.

SCENE THIRTEEN

House. The next day.

The home phone rings.

ZADIE *answers. Maybe we don't see her.*

ZADIE: [*on the phone*] Hello?

> YOLANDI's *voice crackles from the phone, from a faraway place.*

YOLANDI: [*from the phone*] Hi Baba.

> ZADIE *code switches to a South African accent.*

ZADIE: Hi Ma.

YOLANDI: [*from the phone*] How you? You sound—

ZADIE: No, I'm fine, just … tired.

YOLANDI: [*from the phone*] Mmm. Why you never called me back?

ZADIE: Sorry Ma. I should've.

YOLANDI: [*from the phone*] Mm. What you been up to?

ZADIE: Not much.

YOLANDI: [*from the phone*] And Vims?

ZADIE: She's … watching TV.

YOLANDI: [*from the phone*] Everything in the house clean?

ZADIE: Yah. Yah it's clean.

> *Beat.*

Ma … when will you be coming home?

YOLANDI: [*from the phone*] Soon, my child.

> ZADIE *wells up.*

ZADIE: I've done some things, Mama. I've stuffed up. Things I'm not … proud of.

> I've wrecked everything.

YOLANDI: [*from the phone*] What you mean wrecked? Is everyone safe??

ZADIE: No, we're safe. Everything's—

YOLANDI: [*from the phone*] No-one's in jail???

ZADIE: No, no-one's in jail, Ma.

YOLANDI: [*from the phone*] Then what is it?

> *Beat.*

ZADIE: It's … this place, Paradise and the committee, Sharron and—

YOLANDI: [*from the phone*] Oh Zadie. Who cares about the committee?

> ZADIE's *face softens.*

ZADIE: But I thought—?

YOLANDI: [*from the phone*] I don't care about them. Not now. All that matters is y'all are safe and sound. Y'all safe and sound?

A small smile of relief.

ZADIE: Yah …

YOLANDI: [*from the phone*] Good. Zadie, I need you to know about your cousin. You know the one? Stekkie?

ZADIE: Yah. I know the—

YOLANDI: [*from the phone*] She passed away. One week ago. In Joburg.

This news hits ZADIE.

ZADIE: She did …

YOLANDI: [*from the phone*] Yah.

[*Voice breaking*] We're crushed, man. All these years. My heart's just … wishing to rectify with her.

ZADIE: I'm sure hers is too, Ma.

ZADIE *sniffs.*

Hey, I love you.

YOLANDI: [*from the phone*] I love you too, big girl.

SCENE FOURTEEN

Magic Space.

ZADIE *enters with* VIMSY. *She comes forward.* VIMSY *hangs back.*

ZADIE *smiles at us for the first time. She delivers a eulogy.*

ZADIE: My cousin was everything uncontrollable about the world.

She came out of the womb unsure of where she fit. Born to a mumma who didn't want her and a daddy who was a '*no-good, rat-bag-of-a-man*' she was raised in a big house, on a dusty street, by the women around her. By my ma. By my ma's ma. Until sometimes she raised a bit of me.

She was born in the eighties, in a pre-Mandela time when South African law meant mixed relations were illegal. And whether or not Stekkie's dad was white or black or brown was something always in question.

As a result, she had a … wayward, transgression in her blood. And called herself a 'political act' from day dot.

Beat.

She had a habit of dating big, chunky men. Men with beefy shoulders and toothpicks in their mouths type men. She'd bring them home for us to meet, parading them around for all to digest, hanging from their shoulders like a G-string on a clothesline.

ZADIE*'s dialect becomes more South African.*

Stekkie Stekkie Stekkie *Stukkie.*

I know now that *stuk* is Afrikaans for Piece. Piece. Part.

She moved to Joburg when she was twenty-one, twenty-one after saying for years that she was going to get rich quick and '*wipe her bum with fifty-rand notes*'. And one hot, noughties summer morning, as a fuck you to everything *coloured*, everything … constructed by the Apartheid … she hopped on a kombi bus, with a baby in her belly, and fled.

Beat.

I loved her. And found a radiance in her carelessness.

VIMSY *walks up and holds* ZADIE*'s hand.*

My cousin came out of the womb unsure of where she fit. Mixed race and political and radiantly in-between. A child with no place to fit. A woman with no place to fit. A woman who gave and gave … until she had nothing left.

An orange light penetrates the house. Maybe it's radiant and large and all encompassing.

VIMSY: Rest in peace Stekkie.

ZADIE *closes her eyes.*

ZADIE: Rest in peace Stukkie.

The SISTERS *hold each other.*

The light pulses. And then it fades. And STEKKIE *ascends out of life.*

SCENE FIFTEEN

The Rec. Arvo.

LEROY *is sitting at the edge of the pool. Orange speedos, cast on his arm, a huge dick and balls drawn on the cast in permanent marker.*

ZADIE *walks up to* LEROY.

ZADIE: Hey limun trowaaaa.

> LEROY *turns.* ZADIE *notices his arm.*

Far out. Are you okay?

> LEROY *doesn't respond.*

Mind if your dumb crush sits next to you?

> *No response.*

Mind if she explains why she was being really dumb the other day?

> *No response.*

Or if she apologised even?

> ZADIE *sits next to* LEROY.

I feel like I owe you a lot. I have no excuse for how I behaved. For blaming you. For kicking you out. For sabotaging … everything.

> *Beat.*

LEROY: You know Zadie, I've had a lot of time to think with this cast and stuff. And I spoke to Martin and the boys and they were like '*woah*' when I told them what happened. Cos you know what, Zadie? What you did was rough. That was loose behaviour on your part—

ZADIE: I know—

LEROY: No, I'm talking! You've had your time to talk! Now it's my time. [*Beat*] You accused me of vandalising your house. And then I got plaster up to my shoulder and I didn't even hear from you?

> *He looks down at his cast.*

You know I had a competition this weekend? Finals but then I fell flat on my arm, off a roof through a fucking-skylight because I did a dumb thing for the girl I've been in love with for the last five years. And now I have this … crap excuse for an arm and I can't do them. I can't do the finals.

ZADIE: … I didn't realise.

LEROY: You never asked.

> LEROY *musters up some courage.*

Last Sunday, I wasn't at church, I was out the front of yours, in Paradise, standing in fluoro board shorts at eight in the morning because I wanted to see you. But I couldn't wrack up the … nerve. And I've been grappling with some real stuff, Zadie. About my religion, my virginity and—

ZADIE: Wait, you're a virgin?!

LEROY: Yes, I'm a virgin! Of course, I am!

> LEROY *checks over his shoulder.*

[*Whispering*] Sure, I got a wristy when I was sixteen from Hayley Mutton but that doesn't count.

But all that. All that god and injury and sex stuff that's my stuff. I don't go around … swinging, taking on anyone in my path.

ZADIE: I can't believe I …

> ZADIE *musters up some courage.*

You deserved better. I wanna do better. By you. I'm sorry, LiLi.

> *Beat.*

How's the arm?

> *She notices the drawn dick and balls.*

… Is that a dick?

LEROY: I had too much tequila and passed out at Martin's after I got my cast. Turns out guys love drawing penises on those who are—

ZADIE: I'd love your penis.

LEROY: Zadie Peterson.

ZADIE: I mean, if I saw it. I mean I'm sure it's *lovely* and if I saw it—

LEROY: Girl, my eyes are up here.

ZADIE: Stop wearing speedos then! And do you blame me? I can see the circumference from here. Geez.

> *A cute moment.*

> *He leans in softly for a kiss. It's seamless.*

BOOMER WOMAN ON OVERHEAD ANNOUNCEMENT: Ahem. Hate to do this folks but this is the slow lane so if we could keep the heavy petting to a minimum please.

ZADIE: Wanna go back to mine? My parents will be back in a few days so we could take advantage of the free house situationnn?

LEROY: Wait, where are they again?

ZADIE: South Africa!
LEROY: Oh.

> LEROY *punches the air and in the worst South African accent you've ever heard:*

'That's for breaking my TV, bru!'
ZADIE: …What?
LEROY: Blood Diamond? Leonardo DiCapri—
ZADIE: Ohhhhhhhhhhh—
LEROY: 'DeNi Archa!'
ZADIE: Got it.
LEROY: 'T.I.A. This is AfRiCa—

> ZADIE *pashes him again.*

> *These lovebirds get up and run out of The Rec. Hand in hand. Wedgies as they run (?).*

SCENE SIXTEEN

SHARRON: [*voiceover, from machine*] Sadie! What we'd like to do today is to keep you in the loop …
PAUL: [*voiceover, from machine*] The loop is that we've had a meeting. A meeting over at the Paradise Town Hall.
SHARRON: [*voiceover, from machine*] Where residents came forward with any qualms they might have.
PAUL: [*voiceover, from machine*] It gave us—the committee—an opportunity to make a strategy, in Paradise, for the future. As you know a man was in our backyard—
SHARRON: [*voiceover, from machine*] And I'm sure you can appreseeiate that the upkeep of Paradise is very dear to us.
> So we just want to make sure that everyone feels safe.

> *In her bathers,* ZADIE *walks up to the machine. Listens.*

PAUL: [*voiceover, from machine*] Now since the palava of this last week.
SHARRON: [*voiceover, from machine*] We've become concerned that there are unsavoury types coming to the area and—

> ZADIE *presses delete.*

She makes her way out of the house. Into the Paradise sun and onto the roof where VIMSY *is sunbaking, eating an orange. Hair out, bathers bright, sunscreen cheeks.*

ZADIE *gets up and dances on the roof—it's outward and gorgeous and a bit lame.* VIMSY *joins her sibling.*

These two dance over Paradise.

They giggle and twerk and stamp and whip their hair

and hips

and limbs

and bodies

and faces.

The light might look kinda special.

Because they're radiant-like.

STEKKIE-*like.*

THE END

CURTAIN CALL: LL COOL J'S 'PARADISE' could play.

GLOSSARY

COLOURED: Coloureds are a multiracial or mixed ethnic group native to Southern Africa who have ancestry from two or more of the various populations inhabiting the region, including Khoisan, Bantu, Afrikaner, White, Austronesian, East Asian or South Asian people. T

STEKKIE: A slang South African term referring to someone's girlfriend. A referral to a woman as 'a piece'. Derived from the Afrikaans term '*Stukkie*' meaning 'little piece'. '*Stuk*' in Afrikaans: Piece, part. A 'Stekkie' is known for her ghetto and sexy appeal.

EISH: A South African word derived from Xhosa, now used in all languages within South Africa and some neighbouring countries. Used to express a range of emotions, such as surprise, annoyance, or resignation. '*Eish, I never win!*'

SHO: An emphatic expression equivalent to 'wow', 'sure' or 'really?'; as in, '*Sho, it's hot today!*'

SHOO: An exclamation expressing a variety of emotions, especially surprise, wonder, or relief.

CHAP: Originally Afrikaans. Meaning 'guy', 'man'.

WENA: A Zulu word meaning 'you'. Sometimes used in disbelief.

DAGGA: A word used in certain areas of Southern Africa to describe cannabis (Afrikaans pronunciation: [/ˈdaχa/]).

AG, SHAME, MAN: 'Shame' is a typical South African expression for sympathy or admiration. Eg. '*Ag, shame man, poor girl!*' '*Shame, he's so cute.*'

HAIBOH: Derived from the Zulu word meaning 'Definitely not!' This word is usually expressed on its own, at the start or end of a sentence when something seems unbelievable.

YOH: An expression of surprise as in, '*Yoh, that was rude.*' '*Yoh, you gave me a fright!*'

THULA THULA: A traditional African Zulu lullaby.

TWEETY BIRDS: A type of ecstasy pill.

FOOTSACK: Exclamation. South Africa offensive, informal. An expression of dismissal or rejection.

KAK: Borrowed from Afrikaans *kak* ('shit'), from Dutch *kak* ('shit').

RISING STAR

SWEET AND SOUR

COMING-OF-AGE

FFIN THEATRE COMPANY AND RIVERSIDE'S NATIONAL THEATRE OF PARRAMATTA PRESENT

RANGE THROWER

KIRSTY MARILLIER

FEBRUARY – 19 MARCH | SBW STABLES THEATRE

ECTOR
OZI OKENYO

IGNER
EMY ALLEN

HTING DESIGNER
ITY HAMPSON

OCIATE LIGHTING
IGNER
ONIQUE BENETT

COMPOSER &
SOUND DESIGNER
BENJAMIN PIERPOINT

DRAMATURG
DECLAN GREENE

DIRECTING SECONDMENT
CHEMON THEYS

STAGE MANAGER
HANNAH CRANE

WITH
CALLAN COLLEY
ANGELA NICA SULLEN
MARIAMA WHITTON
GABRIELA VAN WYK

IFFIN
EATRE
MPANY

Government partners

NSW

Australian Government

Australia
Council
for the Arts

Co-produced with

RIVERSIDE
NATIONAL THEATRE
of PARRAMATTA

Griffin acknowledges the generosity of the
Seaborn, Broughton & Walford Foundation in
allowing it the use of the SBW Stables Theatre
rent free, less outgoings, since 1986.

PLAYWRIGHT'S NOTE

This play began four years ago. It was the end of 2017, I had just stopped straightening my hair, the word 'diversity' had entered my orbit, but I still didn't believe I could be a playwright.

Orange Thrower is my debut play. It explores a young South African woman's experience living in a stucco suburb called Paradise. I based this fictional place on the drabbest parts of white Australia, areas I was raised in from the years 2000 – 2010 after emigrating from SA.

I thought about the architecture and structure of these places, and how over time, they made me feel stuck. I thought about how they provoked me to assimilate, fracturing my relationship with myself, pushing me into a sad world of internalised racism, tragic hair choices and a decentring of my own Africanness.

I know this sounds a bit grim, but bear with me. I initially wrote *Orange Thrower* in response to a yearning desire to see my own ilk on stage. But after a long and windy road, multiple developments, residencies, and pep talks into believing I could be a playwright, I wrote a work which (I believe) exists as so much more than diverse representation.

Orange Thrower is a summertime play. A chaotic investigation and emotional celebration of womanness, blackness, colouredness, mixedness, otherness, youngness, or any other 'ness' that may feel familiar to one sitting on the margin. It traverses genre, continents, and planes of reality. It's informed by coming-of-age tropes, speaking to Australian greats like *Summer of the Aliens*, *Jasper Jones*, *Away* and *Cloud Street*.

Orange Thrower is a comedy, a mystery, a bonanza of burgeoning sexuality, unrequited love, and risky behaviour. With characters who are my younger selves, older selves, and ancestral selves—sometimes having no clue what to do with their hips, limbs, brains, bodies and faces. I hope you feel them as much as I do.

As a first-time playwright, it's a real gift getting to premiere with Griffin Theatre Company and National Theatre of Parramatta.

My deepest thanks go out to the following Ebony Vagulans, Stephanie Tsindos, Emma O'Sullivan, Aleks Mikic, Ayeesha Ash, Gemma Bird Matheson, Mark Pritchard, Manali Datar, Chika Ikogwe, Kuda Mapeza, Iopu Auva'a, Paula Arundell, Phil Spencer, Lee Lewis, Jessica Arthur, Patrick Jhanur, Candy Bowers, Lucy Ansell, Naomi Rukavina, Rashidi Edwards, 2 Sydney Stylists, Chemon Theys, Tessa Leong.

My love—Tommy Hardham.

My friend who taught me to write— Thomas Wilson-White.

Leila Enright and Courtney Stewart— creative counterparts who spotted me from the start, breathed belief and sense into my work.

Green Door Theatre Company—who developed the first iteration of this play.

The SBW Foundation—who invested in me way back when with the 2019 Rodney Seaborn Playwrights Award.

Polly Rowe, Sydney Theatre Company and their brilliant Rough Draft program.

PLAYWRIGHT'S NOTE

Imogen, Joanne, AJ, and the entirety of Griffin and National Theatre of Parramatta—for reprogramming this show despite lockdown 2.0 being a drag.

Our energetic cast and skilful crew, who have pumped their minds, talents, and imaginations into a bombastic, larger-than-life production.

Declan—theatre hive mind. For every structure doc, every push to redraft, every wild proposition at 6pm on a Friday. I'm a better playwright because of you.

Zindzi—my director, friend, sis and visionary. For bringing my baby to life and for holding my hand at every juncture.

And lastly, my coloured fam—Mum, Dad, Vims and Gigi. For teaching me that no one has my bigness.

Kirsty Marillier
Playwright

DIRECTOR'S NOTE

It's not often you come across a new writer that already possesses such a unique and well-formed writing style. I first came across Kirsty Marillier's work in 2019, playing the role of Stekkie in a development at Sydney Theatre Company. I have never had such a visceral response to a character. Living inside Stekkie's brain was strange and wild, I felt untamed and bound— frightened and yet somehow without fear. When Declan asked me if I wanted to direct this play there was absolutely no doubt in my mind.

Orange Thrower dives into the world of a young coloured South African girl, Zadie, who is striving to fit into the fictional Perth suburb of Paradise. This story moves us through the beating heart of a post-apartheid South African identity— the jagged dreams of assimilation, and the yearning for love and acceptance. Unfortunately, it's a first for a story like this to hit Australian stages, but goodness me now it's here—we are so lucky to have it!

Living in Australia and being African is an... experience. Although the cast and I of course have varied individual feelings towards being African, mixed race or coloured—we all understand on a cellular level the sense of an in-betweenness, a life on the cusp. When you grow up in a country where one of

its states (Queensland, I'm looking at you) created the blueprint for the rules of apartheid, you know exactly what it is to feel other. On the streets, in our relationships, and in our workplaces, we strive to be seen not through a white lens but as our own astounding selves, as all that we are. In the world of *Orange Thrower* we experience these characters' individual journeys as they learn from themselves, the past and ultimately each other.

I'm mindful of saying anything too specific about how you should feel about this work, but what I will say is that if you walk into this theatre with an open mind and heart, you will be moved. Theatre is my favourite medium because it requires us to stop and be present—phones are down and art moves in real time before us. Kirsty Marillier has evoked a world full of joy and resilience that invites every audience member to listen and grow. Oh, and for my black, brown and coloured fam—this one's for you.

Zindzi xx

Zindzi Okenyo
Director

BIOGRAPHIES

KIRSTY MARILLIER WRITER

Kirsty Marillier is a South African/Australian actor and award-winning playwright. She is currently part of the Emerging Writers Group at Sydney Theatre Company and has two original plays in development. Kirsty attended WAAPA, has a BA in Performance Studies and is a proud member of MEAA. Her first work— *Orange Thrower*—was the winner of the 2019 Rodney Seaborn Playwrights Award and her second—*The Zap*—was the winner of the 2020 Max Afford Playwrights Award and was developed with Belvoir St Theatre, Playwriting Australia and Darlinghurst Theatre Company's Next In Line program. Kirsty has been a part of multiple creative programs including Griffin Studio, Sydney Theatre Company's Rough Draft Program (2019), and Malthouse Theatre's Besen Writers Group (2018). In addition to being an award-winning writer, Kirsty is an accomplished performer. Her credits include: for Belvoir: *The Cherry Orchard*; for Black Swan State Theatre Company: *COMA LAND*; for Michael Cassel Group: *Harry Potter and the Cursed Child*; for Sydney Theatre Company: *Home, I'm Darling*. On screen, Kirsty can be seen in *Home and Away*, as well as in the short film *Hook Up*, and feature film *The Greenhouse*. She is thrilled that *Orange Thrower* will have its 2022 premiere with Griffin Theatre Company and National Theatre of Parramatta.

ZINDZI OKENYO DIRECTOR

Zindzi graduated from NIDA in 2006. Her acting credits include: for Griffin: *Girl in Tan Boots*, *Masquerade*; for Bell Shakespeare: *Antony and Cleopatra*, *Much Ado About Nothing*; for Belvoir: *La Traviata*, *Prize Fighter*, *Scorched*; for Darlinghurst Theatre Company: *Gaybies*; for Ensemble Theatre: *Good People*, *The Rasputin Affair*; for Melbourne Theatre Company: *An Ideal Husband*, *The Comedy Of Errors*, *The Crucible*, *The Golden Age*, *The Mysteries: Genesis*, *The Oresteia*, *The Vertical Hour*, *Vs Macbeth*; for State Theatre Company of South Australia: *Random* (for which she won a Curtain Call Award for Best Female Performer); for Sydney Theatre Company: *A History Of Everything*, *Before/After*, *Blood Wedding*, *Boys Will Be Boys*, *Disgraced*, *Grand Horizons*, *Money Shots*; and for Theatre Ink: *Angels in America*. From 2009 to 2011 she was a member of the Residents Company at Sydney Theatre Company. In 2012, Zindzi toured Europe and USA with *A History of Everything* and began as a presenter on ABC's *Play School*. Most recently Zindzi was Co-Director on Darlinghurst Theatre Company's highly acclaimed *seven methods of killing kylie jenner* and Assistant Director for Sydney Theatre Company's *Death of a Salesman*. Zindzi's television roles include: for ABC: *The Code*, *Get Krack!n*, *Harrow*, *Hiding*, *Janet King*, *Play School*, *Wakefield*; and for Network Ten: *Sisters*, *Wonderland*. Zindzi has appeared in the feature films *Little Monsters* and *The Very Excellent Mr Dundee*. Zindzi also performs her own music under the name OKENYO.

JEREMY ALLEN DESIGNER

Jeremy Allen is an Adelaide- and Sydney-based theatre designer. Some of his recent theatre design work includes: for Darlinghurst Theatre Company: *Small Mouth Sounds*; for Hayes Theatre Co: *Merrily We Roll Along*, *The Rise and Disguise of Elizabeth R*; for KXT bAKEHOUSE: *If We Got Some More Cocaine I Could Show You How I Love You*, *Ironbound*; for the National Theatre of Parramatta: *Flight Paths*; for New Theatre: the 2018 Sydney Theatre Award-winning *Stupid Fucking Bird*; for the Old 505: *Home Invasion*; for Pinchgut Opera: *The Loves of Apollo and Dafne*; for Red Line Productions at the Old Fitz: *4:48 Psychosis*, *Angels in America*; for Seymour Centre: *Gloria*, *John*; and for Sydney Theatre Company: *White Pearl*.

VERITY HAMPSON LIGHTING DESIGNER

Verity is a multi-award-winning lighting and projection designer who has designed over 130 productions, working with some of Australia's leading directors and choreographers. For theatre, Verity's designs include: for Griffin: *A Strategic Plan*, *And No More Shall We Part*, *Angela's Kitchen*, *Beached*, *The Bleeding Tree*, *The Boys*, *The Bull, The Moon and the Coronet of Stars*, *Dealing With Clair*, *Dogged*, *The Floating World*, *Superheroes*, *This Year's Ashes*, *The Turquoise Elephant*; for Griffin Independent: *The Brothers Size*, *The Cold Child*, *Crestfall*, *Family Stories: Belgrade*, *Live Acts On Stage*, *Music*, *The New Electric Ballroom*, *References to Salvador Dali Make Me Hot*, *Way to Heaven*; for Griffin and Bell Shakespeare: *The Literati*; for Bell Shakespeare: *A Midsummer Night's Dream*, *Julius Caesar*, *Titus Andronicus*; for Belvoir: *An Enemy of the People*, *The Drover's Wife*, *Faith Healer*, *Winyanboga Yurringa*; for CAAP/Sydney Festival: *Double Delicious*; for Dancenorth: *Dungarri Nya Nya Ngarri Bi Nya*; for Ensemble Theatre: *Baby Doll*, *Fully Committed*; for Hayes Theatre Co: *Lizzie*; for Malthouse Theatre: *Wake in Fright*; for Queensland Theatre: *Death of a Salesman*; and for Sydney Theatre Company: *7 Stages of Grieving*, *Blackie Blackie Brown*, *Grand Horizons*, *Hamlet: Prince of Skidmark*, *Home, I'm Darling*, *Machinal*, *Little Mercy*. Verity is a recipient of the Mike Walsh Fellowship; three Sydney Theatre Awards; a Green Room Award; and an APDG Award for Best Lighting Design.

VERONIQUE BENETT ASSOCIATE LIGHTING DESIGNER

Veronique is a lighting, set and costume designer. Veronique holds a Master of Fine Art (Design for Performance) majoring in lighting and a Bachelor of Fine Art (Technical Theatre and Stage Management) from NIDA. As lighting designer, Veronique's credits include: for Griffin: *The Smallest Hour*; for Circa: *Sacre*; for Hayes Theatre Co: *The Life of Us*; for KXT bAKEHOUSE: *A Girl is a Half-formed Thing*; for New Theatre: *Stupid Fucking Bird*; for the Old 505: *Nosferatu*; for Outhouse Theatre Co: *John* (for which she was nominated for a Sydney Theatre Award for Best Lighting Design of an Independent Production); for Red Line Productions at the Old Fitz: *Anatomy of a Suicide*, *Chorus*, *Happy Days* (for which she was nominated for a Sydney Theatre Award for Best Lighting Design of an Independent Production), *Howie the Rookie*, *Permission to Spin*; and for Sydney

Theatre Company: *Banging Denmark*. Veronique's associate lighting design credits include: for Griffin: *Prima Facie*; for Belvoir: *Cursed!*; for Hayes Theatre Co: *Cry-Baby*; for Sport for Jove: *A Midsummer Night's Dream*, *Macbeth*, *The Tempest*; and for Sydney Theatre Company: *No Pay? No Way!*. As set and lighting designer, Veronique's credits include: for Red Line Productions at the Old Fitz: *Exit the King* (for which she was nominated for a Sydney Theatre Award for Best Stage Design of an Independent Production); for Outhouse Theatre Co: *Ulster American* (for which she was nominated for a Sydney Theatre Award for Best Stage Design of an Independent Production); and for NIDA: *Venus in Fur*. Veronique was the costume and lighting designer for NIDA's *Women on the Verge of a Nervous Breakdown*.

BENJAMIN PIERPOINT COMPOSER & SOUND DESIGNER

Ben is a theatremaker, live performance producer/director, composer and sound designer. Ben began composing and sound designing with Clockfire Theatre Company as an Artistic Associate in 2013, collaborating on their shows: *A Hunger Suite*, *The Grief Parlour*, *The Natural Conservatorium for Wise Women* and *we, the lost company*. Other credits include: for Apocalypse Theatre Company: *Angels in America*, *Asylum*, *Doubt: A Parable*, *Lady Tabouli*, *Metamorphoses* (for which he won a Sydney Theatre Award), *Omar and Dawn*; for Empress Theatre: *Cyprus Avenue*; for Glitterbomb in association with 25A: *Extinction of the Learned Response*, *The Maids*; for JackRabbit Theatre Company: *A Little Piece of Ash;* for the Joan Sutherland Performing Arts Centre: *Black Birds*; for Mad March Hare: *You Got Older*; for Mad March Hare/Outhouse Theatre Company: *Dry Land;* for Mophead Productions: *Fierce*; for National Theatre of Parramatta: *The Girl/The Woman*; for Outhouse Theatre Company: *Gloria*; for Red Line Productions at the Old Fitz: *Degenerate Art*; for Sugary Rum in association with 25A: *Jess & Joe Forever*. Since 2015, Ben has worked with four-time ARIA Award-nominated artist NGAIIRE on multiple projects, along with leading the management teams of future-soul vocalist Wallace, hip hop artist Jamaica Moana, film and dance composer Nick Wales and Yorta Yorta musician and poet Allara.

DECLAN GREENE DRAMATURG

Declan is the Artistic Director of Griffin Theatre Company and works as a playwright, dramaturg and director. As director, his credits include: for Griffin: *Dogged*, *Green Park*; for Malthouse Theatre: *Wake in Fright*; for Malthouse Theatre/Sydney Theatre Company: *Blackie Blackie Brown*; for Sydney Theatre Company: *Hamlet: Prince of Skidmark*; for ZLMD Shakespeare Company: *Conviction*. As playwright, his work includes *Eight Gigabytes of Hardcore Pornography*, *The Homosexuals, or 'Faggots'*, *Melancholia*, *Moth*, and *Pompeii L.A.* Declan co-founded queer experimental theatre company Sisters Grimm with Ash Flanders in 2006, and has directed and co-created all their productions to date, including: for Griffin Independent and Theatre Works: *Summertime in the Garden of Eden*; for Malthouse Theatre and Sydney Theatre Company: *Calpurnia Descending*; for Melbourne Theatre Company: *Lilith: The Jungle Girl*; and for Sydney Theatre Company: *Little Mercy*. He was previously Resident Artist at Malthouse Theatre.

CHEMON THEYS DIRECTING SECONDMENT

Chemon graduated from NIDA in 2017 and their acting credits include: for Bontom: *Chorus*; for Little Eggs Collective at KXT bAKEHOUSE: *Symphonie Fantastique*; for NIDA: *Antigonick*; for Sydney Chamber Opera/Sydney Festival: *Future Remains*. Chemon's television credits include Binge's *Deadly Women*. Chemon was a feature voice actor for *Haunted House*, a gaming project for Endless Adventures, and most recently voiced the role of Frankenstein's Bride in the Universal Pictures/Fortnite short-form mini-series: *We Will Be Monsters*. Chemon is currently in the ensemble for the Australian tour of *Girl from the North Country*.

This role is generously supported by members of the Griffin Women's Initiative.

HANNAH CRANE STAGE MANAGER

Hannah Crane is a self-taught stage manager working on unceded Gadigal and Darug land. Hannah's theatre credits include: for Griffin: *Wherever She Wanders*; for Apocalypse Theatre Company: *All My Sleep and Waking*, *Angels in America*, *Omar and Dawn*; for Hasemann, Ball, & Radda: *The Serpent's Teeth*; for Lambert House Productions: *Jasper Jones*; for National Theatre of Parramatta: *Lady Tabouli*, *The Sorry Mum Project*, *Zombie Thoughts*; for Thirty-Five Square: *Duckpond*. She is a graduate of the University of Sydney (B.A.).

CALLAN COLLEY LEROY/SHARRON

Callan is a NIDA graduate and an accomplished actor on stage. His theatre credits include: for Melbourne Theatre Company: *Gloria;* for Sydney Theatre Company: *Death of a Salesman*, *Three Sisters*. Callan stars in the upcoming feature film *Dark Noise*, and on television he can be seen in Season 2 of ABC/Netflix's *The Let Down*.

ANGELA NICA SULLEN STEKKIE/PAUL

Angela Nica Sullen is an Italian, African American woman from the United States. She grew up in California and on Noongar country in Western Australia. Angela is an actor, vocal coach, writer, MC and self-proclaimed comedian. Now based on Gadigal land, she studied at the National Institute of Dramatic Art, completing a Bachelor of Fine Arts (Acting) and a Master of Fine Arts (Voice). Her theatre credits include: for Black Birds/Griffin Theatre Company's Batch Festival/Darlinghurst Theatre Company's Festival Fatale/ Red Line Productions at the Old Fitz: *Brown Skin Girl*; for Australian Chamber Orchestra in association with Belvoir: *Bridgetower*; for Force Majeure: *Nothing To Lose*; for the Old 505: *The House at Boundary Road, Liverpool*; and for Sydney Theatre Company: *Mosquitoes*. Her vocal and dialect coaching credits include: for Darlinghurst Theatre Company: *seven methods of killing kylie jenner*; for NIDA: *God's Country*; and for Sydney Theatre Company: *Grand Horizons*. Angela's television credits include: for Stan: *Bump*; for NBC: *La Brea*; and she can be seen in the feature film *I Am Woman*. Angela is currently an Associate Lecturer for Voice at the National Institute of Dramatic Art and is also working on *Seen*, a new television series produced by Rough Diamond, inspired by *Brown Skin* Girl, a play she collaborated on with creative collective Black Birds.

MARIAMA WHITTON VIMSY

Mariama Whitton is an actor and voice over artist who was adopted from Ethiopia when she was three years old. In 2019, and she graduated from the Western Australian Academy of Performing Arts (WAAPA). Prior to WAAPA she completed her ATCL (Associate Trinity College of London) in performing, as well as courses at NIDA, ACA, and the Hub Studio. Her theatre credits include: for WAAPA: *Birdland, Bullies*, *The Misanthrope*, *Romeo & Juliet*, *The Seagull*. On screen, Mariama can be seen in the short film *The Docks*.

GABRIELA VAN WYK ZADIE

Gabriela is a proud South African-Australian actor based in Meanjin. She is a recent graduate from Queensland University of Technology's Bachelor of Fine Arts (Acting). After graduation, she hopes to pursue a career on stage and screen. Gabriela has experience as a freelance model, singer and songwriter, she hugely admires the likes of Zendaya, Viola Davis and Michaela Coel—three powerhouse women of colour whose storytelling inspires change. Her recent theatre roles include: for Queensland University of Technology: *Algorithm*, *Children of the Sun*, *Gloria*, *Twelfth Night*.

ABOUT GRIFFIN

Griffin is the only theatre company in the country exclusively devoted to the development and staging of new Australian writing. Located in the historic SBW Stables Theatre, nestled in the heart of Kings Cross, Griffin has been Australia's home for the exploration of new stories since 1978.

We are the launch pad for new plays, ideas and writing that other theatres won't take a risk on. We boldly contribute to Australia's unique and powerful storytelling culture. Plays like *Prima Facie*, *Holding the Man* and *City of Gold* all had their world premieres at Griffin before going out to capture the national imagination. In the words of our longest-serving Artistic Director, **Ros Horin**:

"We are the theatre of first chances."

We are passionate about nurturing emerging and established practitioners alike. We pride ourselves on supporting our vast community of artists, audiences and supporters who consider our theatre their creative home. We help ambitious, bold, risk-taking and urgent Australian work get from the page onto the stage. We tell the stories that help us know who we are as a nation, and who we want to become.

Acknowledgement of Country

Griffin Theatre Company and the SBW Stables Theatre operate and tell stories on the unceded lands of the Gadigal of the Eora Nation. We acknowledge and honour Aboriginal and Torres Strait Islander people as the oldest continuous living culture on the planet, with more than 60,000 years of storytelling practice shaping and underpinning all aspects of Australian culture. It is a privilege that we do not take lightly: to work on this land, and to tell stories on its soil.

GRIFFIN THEATRE COMPANY
13 Craigend St
Kings Cross NSW 2011

02 9332 1052
info@griffintheatre.com.au
griffintheatre.com.au

SBW STABLES THEATRE
10 Nimrod St
Kings Cross NSW 2011

BOOKINGS
griffintheatre.com.au
02 9361 3817

GRIFFIN FAMILY

Patron
Seaborn, Broughton &
Walford Foundation
*Griffin acknowledges the
generosity of the Seaborn,
Broughton & Walford
Foundation in allowing it
the use of the SBW Stables
Theatre rent free, less
outgoings, since 1986.*

Board
Bruce Meagher (Chair),
Simon Burke AO, Lyndell
Droga, Tim Duggan,
Declan Greene, Mario
Philippou, Julia Pincus,
Lenore Robertson, Simone
Whetton, Meyne Wyatt

Artistic Director & CEO
Declan Greene

Executive Director & CEO
Julieanne Campbell

Associate Artistic Director
Tessa Leong

Associate Artist
Andrea James

Literary Associate
Julian Larnach

Box Office Manager
Dominic Scarf

Bar Manager
Grace Nye-Butler

Front of House
Bridget Haberecht, Julian
Larnach, Poppy Tidswell

**Associate Producer,
Development**
Frankie Greene

Development Coordinator
Ell Katte

Finance Manager
Kylie Richards

Finance Consultant
Emma Murphy

**Associate Producer,
Marketing**
AJ Lamarque

Marketing Coordinator
Ang Collins

Marketing Assistant
Rebecca Abdel-Messih

Production Manager
Jeremy Page

Production Coordinator
Ally Moon

Senior Producer
Imogen Gardam

**Administration &
Programs Manager**
Whitney Richards

**Strategic Insights
Consultant**
Peter O'Connell

**Sustainability
Coordinators**
Ang Collins,
Grace Nye-Butler

Brand & Graphic Design
Alphabet

Web Developer
DevQuoll

Cover Photography
Brett Boardman

GRIFFIN DONORS

Income from Griffin activities covers less than 40% of our operating costs—leaving an ever-increasing gap for us to fill through government funding, sponsorship and the generosity of our individual supporters. Your support helps us bridge the gap and keep ticket prices affordable and our work at its best. To make a donation and a difference, contact Griffin on **9332 1052** or donate online at **griffintheatre.com.au**

COMPANY PATRONS
Neilson Foundation

PRODUCTION PATRONS
Girgensohn Foundation

PROGRAM PATRONS

Griffin Ambassadors
Robertson Foundation

Griffin Studio
Gil Appleton
Darin Cooper Foundation
Kiong Lee & Richard Funston
Rosemary Hannah & Lynette Preston
Ken & Lilian Horler
Malcolm Robertson Foundation
Pip Rath & Wayne Lonergan
Geoff & Wendy Simpson OAM
Danielle Smith & Sean Carmody
Walking up the Hill Foundation

Griffin Studio Workshop
Mary Ann Rolfe (Patron)
Bob Ernst
Susan MacKinnon
Pip Rath & Wayne Lonergan

Griffin Women's Initiative
Anonymous (1)
Katrina Barter
Wendy Blacklock
Christy Boyce & Madeleine Beaumont
Julieanne Campbell
Iolanda Capodanno
Laura Crennan
Jennifer Darin
Lyndell Droga

Melinda Graham
Sherry Gregory
Rosemary Hannah & Lynette Preston
Antonia Haralambis
Ann Johnson
Roanne Knox
Susan MacKinnon
Julia Pincus
Ruth Ritchie
Lenore Robertson
Sonia Simich
Deanne Weir
Simone Whetton

Griffin Women's Initiative was originally supported by Creative Partnerships Australia through Plus1.

SEASON PATRONS
As a new writing theatre, we program a wide range of stories that reflect our time, place and the unique voice of contemporary Australia. To ensure that these stories continue to be told, Griffin needs the help of private support to bring strength, insight, candour and new and powerful visions to the stage. Our Production Partner program is vital to our continued artistic success.

PRODUCTION PARTNERS 2021

***Dogged* by Andrea James & Catherine Ryan**
Lisa Barker & Don Russell
Darin Cooper Foundation
Robert Dick & Erin Shiel

Lyndell & Daniel Droga
Danny Gilbert AM & Kathleen Gilbert
Rosemary Hannah & Lynette Preston
Bruce Meagher & Greg Waters
Richard McHugh & Kate Morgan
Julia Pincus & Ian Learmonth
Pip Rath & Wayne Lonergan

SEASON DONORS

Company Patron $100,000+
Neilson Foundation

Season Patron $50,000+
Girgensohn Foundation

Mainstage Donors $20,000+
Robert Dick & Erin Shiel
Rosemary Hannah & Lynette Preston
Julia Pincus & Ian Learmonth
Robertson Foundation
Mary Ann Rolfe

Production Donors $10,000+
Anonymous (1)
Lisa Barker & Don Russell
Darin Cooper Foundation
Gordon & Marie Esden
Abraham & Helen James
Ingrid Kaiser
Richard McHugh & Kate Morgan
Bruce Meagher & Greg Waters
Peter & Dianne O'Connell
Pip Rath & Wayne Lonergan

GRIFFIN DONORS

The WeirAnderson
Foundation
Kim Williams AM and
Catherine Dovey

Rehearsal Donors
$5,000 – $9,999
Anonymous (1)
Antoinette Albert
Gil Appleton
Wendy Blacklock
Ellen Borda
Susan Carleton
Bernard Coles
Ian Dickson
Lyndell & Daniel Droga
Danny Gilbert AM &
Kathleen Gilbert
Ken & Lilian Horler
Lambert Bridge Foundation
Kiong Lee & Richard Funston
Lee Lewis & Brett Boardman
Sophie McCarthy &
Antony Green
Catriona Morgan-Hunn
Anthony Paull
Rebel Penfold-Russell OAM
Geoff & Wendy Simpson OAM
The Sky Foundation
Merilyn Sleigh &
Raoul de Ferranti
Danielle Smith & Sean
Carmody
Walking Up the Hill
Foundation

Final Draft Donors
$3,000 – $4,999
Jocelyn Goyen
Sherry Gregory
James Hartwright &
Kerrin D'Arcy
Roanne & John Knox
Don & Leslie Parsonage
Leslie Stern

Workshop Donors
$1,000 – $2,999
Anonymous (4)
Baly Douglass Foundation
Katrina Barter
Helen Bauer &
Helen Lynch AM
Cherry & Peter Best
Christy Boyce & Madeleine
Beaumont
Dr Bernadette Brennan
Anne Britton
Corinne & Bryan
Stephen & Annabelle Burley
Julieanne Campbell
Iolanda Capodanno
Louise Christie
Anna Cleary
Bryony & Tim Cox
Sally Crawford
Laura Crennan
Cris Croker & David West
Bob Ernst
Ros & Paul Espie
Brian Everingham
Jan Ewert
John & Libby Fairfax
Sandra Forbes
Jennifer Giles
Nicky Gluyas
Melinda Graham
Peter Gray & Helen Thwaites
Antonia Haralambis
Kate Harrison
John Head
Libby Higgin
Mark Hopkinson &
Michelle Opie
Michael Jackson
Ann Johnson
David & Adrienne Kitching
Elizabeth Laverty
Benjamin Law
Richard & Elizabeth Longes
Kyrsty Macdonald &
Christopher Hazell
Susan MacKinnon

Prudence Manrique
Lorin Muhlmann
Jane Munro
David Nguyen
Ian Phipps
Martin Portus
Annabel Ritchie
In memory of Katherine
Robertson
Sylvia Rosenblum
Sonia Simich
Jann Skinner
Stuart Thomas
Elizabeth Thompson
Mike Thompson
Sue Thomson
Janet Wahlquist
Richard Weinstein &
Richard Benedict
Simone Whetton
Rob White & Lisa Hamilton
Rosemary White
Paul & Jennifer Winch
Elizabeth Wing

Reading Donors
$500 – $999
Anonymous (3)
Brian Abel
Priscilla Adey
Jane Albert
Amity Alexander
Wendy Ashton
Robyn Ayres
Melissa Ball
Phillip Black
Larry Boyd &
Barbara Caine AM
Tim Capelin
Michael Diamond AM MBE
Max Dingle OAM
Elizabeth Diprose
David Earp
Leonie Flannery
Alan Froude & David Round
Peter Graves
Erica Gray
Stephanie & Andrew Harrison

GRIFFIN DONORS

David Hoskins & Paul McKnight
Sylvia Hrovatin
Nicki Jam
Mira Joksovic
Matt Jones & Rebecca Bourne Jones
Colleen Mary Kane
Susan J Kath
Patricia Lynch
Ian & Elizabeth MacDonald
Suzanne & Anthony Maple-Brown
Robert Marks
Chris Marrable & Kate Richardson
Simon Marrable & Anna Kasper
Christopher Matthies
Christopher McCabe
John McCallum & Jenny Nicholls
Daniela McMurdo
Jacqui Mercer
John Mitchell
Neville Mitchell
Keith Moynihan
Patricia Novikoff
Carolyn Penfold
Belinda Piggott & David Ojerholm
Virginia Pursell
Alex-Oonagh Redmond
Karen Rodgers & Bill Harris
Gemma Rygate
Rob & Rae Spence
Mary Stollery & Eric Dole
Catherine Sullivan & Alexandra Bowen
Ariadne Vromen
Robyn Fortescue & Rosie Wagstaff
Helen Wicker

**First Draft Donors
$200-$499**
Anonymous (9)
Susan Ambler

Elizabeth Antonievich
William Armitage
Chris Baker
Jan Barr
John Bell AO, OBE
Edwina Birch
Andrew Bowmer
Peter Brown
Wendy Buswell
Ruth Campbell
David Caulfield
Amanda Clark
Sue Clark
Louise Costanzo
Brendan Crotty & Darryl Toohey
Bryan Cutler
Sue Donnelly
Peter Duerden
Anna Duggan
Kathy Esson
Elizabeth Evatt
Michael Eyers
Helen Ford
Judith Fox
Eva Gerber
Jock Given
Deane Golding
Keith Gow
Virginia & Kieran Greene
Jo Grisard
Edwina Guinness
Ruth Guss
Kate Haddock
Raewyn Harlock
Robert Henderson & Marijke Conrade
Grania Hickley
Matthew Huxtable
Marian & Nabeel Ibrahim
Andrew Inglis
James Landon-Smith
Penelope Latey
Liz Locke
Danielle Long
Norman Long
Noella Lopez
Maruschka Loupis

Anni MacDougall
Claire McCaughan
Louise McDonald
Duncan McKay
Paula McLean
Stephen McNamara
Anne Miehs
Julia Mitchell
Mark Mitchell
Sarah Mort
Margaret Murphy
Carolyn Newman
Suzanne Osmond
Catherine & Joshua Palmer
Peter Pezzutti
Christopher Powell
Janelle Prescott
Andrew Pringle
Dorothy & Adit Rao
Tracey Robson
Ann Rocca
Catherine Rothery
Kevin and Shirley Ryan
Dimity Scales
Julia Selby
Natalie Shea
Vivienne Skinner
Bridget Smith
Vanda and Martin Smith
Augusta Supple
Danny Tomic
Rachel Trigg
Samantha Turley
Adam Van Rooijen
Julie Whitfield
Eve Wynhausen
Robert Yuen
William Zappa

We would also like to thank Peter O'Connell for his expertise, guidance, and time.

**Current as of
10 January 2022**

SPONSORS

Griffin would like to thank the following:

OUR PARTNERS

Government Supporters   Benefactor

Australian Government | Australia Council for the Arts

NSW GOVERNMENT

CITY OF SYDNEY

SBW Foundation

Creative Partners

alphabet.

Brett Boardman Photography

COPYRIGHT AGENCY CULTURAL FUND

GIRGENSOHN FOUNDATION

MALCOLM ROBERTSON FOUNDATION

NEILSON FOUNDATION

PLAYKING FOUNDATION

ROBERTSON FOUNDATION

Company Sponsors

Beppi's
Established 1956

Bourke street bakery

CURRENCY PRESS

PROUDLY EST. 2014
FOUR PILLARS
SMALL AUSTRALIAN DISTILLERY

MARQUE

MOPPITY Vineyards

Rosenfeld, Kant & Co.
Business & Financial Solutions

SATURDAY PAPER

THE UNIVERSITY OF SYDNEY

Griffin Theatre Company is assisted by the Australian Government through the Australia Council, its arts funding and advisory body; and the NSW Government through Create NSW.

www.currency.com.au

Visit Currency Press' website now to:

- Order books
- Browse through our full list of titles including plays, screenplays, theory and reference/criticism, performance handbooks, educational texts and more
- Choose a play for your school or performance group by cast specs
- Seek performance rights
- Find out about performing arts news and sign up for our newsletter
- For students: read our study guides
- For teachers: access free curriculum information and teacher notes

We are also on Facebook and Instagram (@currencypress). Join the conversation!

The performing arts publisher

www.ingramcontent.com/pod-product-compliance
Lightning Source LLC
Chambersburg PA
CBHW050020090426
42734CB00021B/3355